Life Is a Self-Designed, Personal Growth Seminar

Rebecca L. Morgan, CSP, CMC

Life Is a Self-Designed, Personal Growth Seminar

©2019 Rebecca L. Morgan

All rights reserved. No part of this book may be reproduced or transmitted in any form or by any means, electronic or mechanical, including photocopying, recording, or by any information storage or retrieval system, without the written permission from the copyright holder, except for the inclusion of quotations in a review.

Printed in the United States of America.
ISBN: 978-1-930039-62-9

How to order:
Quantity copies may be ordered directly from
www.RebeccaMorgan.com.

Go to RebeccaMorgan.com/life for updates and other resources.

How to Use This Book

This unique book is comprised of Rebecca's original photos from her world travels coupled with her thought-provoking essays based on her observations. It is designed for you to first read and think about each image's quote and how you can use it in your life. Then read the accompanying essay that elaborates the main point.

This book is intended to either reinforce, or pivot your thinking.

You'll get more out of this if you take a few minutes to write down your thoughts on how to use the concepts.

How to use this book

+ *Determine how you can use ideas:* A concept put into action has much more value than just knowing the idea.

+ *Learn from "OPE" — Other People's Experiences:* If you're astute, you learn from your own life experiences. Some of these are positive — some are negative. It is less painful to learn from other people's unpleasant experiences!

+ *Share with others:* Read and discuss the ideas at your staff meetings or dinner table Facilitate a discussion to adapt the lessons to help each person become more effective.

Books by Rebecca L. Morgan

Leadership Lessons from Silicon Valley: How to Survive and Thrive in Disruptive Times

Calming Upset Customers: Stay in Control ... in Any Situation

Grow Your Key Talent: Thought-Provoking Essays for Business Owners, Executives and Managers on Developing Star Staff

Life's Lessons: Insights and Information for a Richer Life

Professional Selling: Practical Secrets for Successful Sales

Remarkable Customer Service ... and Disservice: Case Studies and Discussions to Increase Your Customers' Delight

All can be ordered at
www.RebeccaMorgan.com

About the Author

Rebecca L. Morgan is an internationally recognized consultant, trainer, facilitator, and speaker, based in San José, CA.

Rebecca partners with clients to create innovative, long-lasting professional development solutions. Her focus is on leadership development implementation, strategic customer service, and increasing workplace effectiveness by providing the right skills for the right people in the right way.

Many recognizable organizations have engaged Rebecca to develop creative solutions to their situations. These include: Apple, Singapore Airlines, Wells Fargo Bank, New York Life Insurance, Microsoft, ING, Hewlett-Packard, Adobe, Hyatt Hotels, Applied Materials, Quantum, Seagate, Sun Microsystems, Lockheed Martin, Sony, and Stanford University, among many more.

Rebecca is a respected professional development consultant, best-selling author, and speaker.

Her media appearances include 60 Minutes, The Oprah Winfrey Show, National Public Radio's Market Place, *USA Today*, *Wall Street Journal*, Forbes.com, *San José Mercury News*, Malaysia's *Star* newspaper, Singapore's *Straight Times*, the *Brunei Times*, *The Asian Journal*, and the *San Francisco Chronicle*. Her ideas are so solid that Microsoft hired her as its workplace effectiveness spokesperson.

Rebecca's books, recordings, videos, and learning tools exemplify the excellence she creates in all of her work. She's authored 28 popular books — two of which have been translated into nine languages.

One of an Elite Few Professionals

Rebecca is committed to continuous learning and growing, especially since that is what she imparts to others. She has demonstrated this striving by receiving the Certified Speaking Professional (CSP) designation conferred by the National Speakers Association (NSA). At the time, the ten-year-old designation had been earned by only 215 people in the world—less than seven percent of the 3700 members of NSA.

She has also earned the professional designation Certified Management Consultant (CMC) from the Institute of Management Consultants (IMC). She is the fifteenth professional in the world to earn both the CSP and the CMC designations.

Go to www.RebeccaMorgan.com for more information on Rebecca's services.

Contents

Introduction 1

Life Is a Self-Designed, Personal Growth Seminar 3

Is Your Self-Reliance Dooming You? 7

Say "Yes" to Beckoning Adventures 11

Are You Difficult? 15

Act on Your Curiosity 19

Your Conscientiousness Determines Your Success 23

A Cup Of Coffee Lasts 40 Years 27

Dependability Is a Superpower 31

Stop Offering Feedback 35

Eschew Frivolous Talk. Seek Meaningful Conversation 39

The Path to Wisdom 43

Be a Conscious Conversationalist 47

Humor, at Someone Else's Expense, Can Cut More Deeply Than You'll Ever Know 53

Become A Time-Conscious Communicator 57

Venting Is Toxic 61

Eight Lessons Learned from a Bali Girls Home 65

Don't Make Decisions for Me Without Consulting Me 71

Don't Focus on Reaching Your Goals 75

Leaderful Listening 79

Take Calculated Risks 83

Stand Out As a True Professional 89

Is Your Superpower Recognizing Others' Superpowers? 93

Same-o, Same-o is Lame-o, Lame-o. Embrace Your Uniqueness! 97

Cultivate Many Mini-Mentors 101

Harness the Power of Commitment 105

Honesty, Without Caring, Is Abuse 109

Give Verbal Hugs 113

Vulnerability + Strength = Personal Power 115

Commit to Continuous Personal Improvement 119

Practice Microconnections Every Day 123

Two Magic Words to Cool Tense Situations 127

Waves Are Like People 131

A Formula for Growth 135

Couple Candor with Kindness 139

Resources 141

Introduction

This book is designed around key lessons I've learned in my life that have molded who I am. I often sprinkle these into my business seminars when relevant to the topic.

Recently, I coupled the sayings with some of my favorite photos snapped during my worldwide travels. I have no delusions of being an expert photographer. I'm just someone who enjoys finding unusual shots that catch my eye. Sometimes the photos pertain to the quote; sometimes not. I wanted to pair an interesting visual with a (hopefully) interesting thought.

The quote graphic is combined with an essay elaborating the quote.

My goal is to offer some thought-provoking fodder for you to ponder. If you like the sentiment, then strive to integrate it into your life.

If you think the idea is worth sharing, it may make for a rich discussion at your next staff meeting or family dinner. If you allow people to freely share their thinking on the quote, a insightful conversation can ensure.

The image quotes are also available as postcards and posters if you'd like visual reminders. You may want to post them in your workspace, or to share in your work hallway or break room. At home, you can post them on your refrigerator, bathroom mirror, or bedroom door. The postcards are designed for you can send to someone you think would appreciate the message.

Optimally, you choose a different message each week to discuss with your team or family. By switching them each week, you can create an environment where people are continually striving to improve themselves.

Life is a self-designed, personal growth seminar.

Seek lessons from each experience.

©Rebecca Morgan, CSP, CM
www.RebeccaMorgan.co

How can you apply this concept?

_____

_____

_____

_____

_____

Life Is a Self-Designed, Personal Growth Seminar

Our lives have incredible highs and some heartbreaking lows. The former are exhilarating. You think, "How can life get any better?"

The lows can involve blaming ourselves, feeling stupid, and being embarrassed for our part in the mishap. Or we condemn others, thinking they caused this setback.

The difference between those who rebound quickly and those who linger in their negativity is their perspective. Wallowers stay stuck in victimhood, never reflecting on the lesson the experience has for them.

The sooner you can shift from anger or sadness to introspection, the happier you will be. Every disappointment has a gift for you, if you are willing to look for it. This is not always easy. The more time distancing you from the event, the easier it gets. However, if you can train yourself to look for the lesson as soon after the event as possible, the less suffering you'll have.

It took me many years to learn to speedily find value in disappointments. Sometimes it still takes me longer than I'd like. When I've shifted my perspective quickly, the wiser and more at peace I've become.

When I'm able to look for the lessons, I'm reminded of the many personal growth workshops I've attended. These are typically full of exercises confronting your thinking and behavior, then teaching you new perspectives so you can shift your paradigm. You become a "participant observer" to your life — able to reflect on your behaviors soon after the event.

This is especially helpful if you are trying to change a habit. For example, I would get attention by cutting humor targeting those around me. Others would laugh, including, sometimes, the target of my "teasing." However, I noticed that when others would tease me similarly, putting me down for laughs, it didn't feel good. It felt hurtful. I realized I was doing this to others. I asked myself, "Do I want to destroy my relationships, or strengthen them? The answer was easy — to make them stronger.

I observed that I had caused or contributed to the vast majority of mishaps in my life. Not all, of course, but a great percentage of them. I then realized that I was designing a personal growth seminar — my life. I would keep having similar disappointments until I learned the lesson and didn't repeat the same behavior. The sooner I had the epiphany, the sooner I'd integrate the insight. It would reduce my suffering, and make me a better person.

Reflect on some of the setbacks in your life. Have you unearthed the lesson? Or are you still blaming yourself or others, not acknowledging the hand you had in creating it? If the event was beyond your control or not, what did you learn about yourself that you can carry forward? If nothing else, you can learn to forgive yourself and others quickly.

Thinking of your life as a self-designed, personal growth seminar gives you more power, as you see that you have more control than you might think. Instead of blame, you shift to asking, "What lesson do I need to learn from this?" That's a place of peace.

Seek lessons from each experience.

> *Every disappointment has a gift for you*

About the Photo

I took this photo at Wat Mahathat, a Buddhist temple in Ayutthaya, Thailand, about an hour's drive north of Bangkok. It contains the ruins of the old capital city of the Ayutthaya Kingdom.

This head of the Buddha statue has sunk into the ground while the tree grew up around it. The image is striking.

I wasn't excited about going to Ayutthaya, but my traveling buddy, Ava, loves to photograph ruins. We had two days before leaving for our next stop, and Ayutthaya was close to Bangkok where we had been staying for a few days. So I agreed to accompany her.

We settled into our guest house, then began our adventure to the Wat Mahathat. There was not only this interesting Buddha stature encircled by a tree, there were other ruins, with some parts well preserved. Some have been restored.

I took refuge on a shady bench as the hot sun was oppressive. I'd taken the photos I wanted, but Ava was still clicking away.

Near me, a young man left his parents in the same tree's cool shelter. Overhearing their conversation, I discerned they were Japanese.

Wanting a connection, I remembered a few words from my college Japanese. I could really only say, "How are you?" At first they seemed puzzled, not really expecting me to speak any Japanese. But they smiled and replied.

Unfortunately, I couldn't translate. So we just smiled and nodded.

Having made even a minimal connection made the wait with these strangers more pleasant. I'm glad I tried.

Heed others' wisdom and experience.

It can save you from self-destructing.

©Rebecca Morgan, CSP, CMC
www.RebeccaMorgan.com

How can you apply this concept?

_____

_____

_____

_____

_____

Is Your Self-Reliance Dooming You?

A pal has been a supervisor at our local hardware store for eight years. He shared a story about Eric, the new general manager — someone who'd never worked in a hardware store and was hired 6 months ago.

Eric is a nice guy, but he doesn't see how he's causing himself to fail. It appears that Eric has a lot of confidence since he never asks anyone else for input. The result is a messy store, frustrated staff and irritated customers. The store sales numbers are suffering as a result.

For example, the store gets sale signs and merchandise from the home office far in advance of the sale. But Eric doesn't assign people to put up the signs and put out the merchandise until the last day of the sale.

> *He doesn't see how he's causing himself to fail*

Customers come in looking for the sale items and either leave when they can't find it or have to ask a staff member. The latter then has to go in the back and search through the boxes to find what is needed.

Prior to Eric's arrival, Harry, the former manager, would ensure the sale items and signs were in a place designated for upcoming sales. The night before the sale was launched, Harry would assign a few people to post the signs and put the items in a prominent spot in the appropriate sections. Customers and staff could then easily find what the ad promoted.

Eric also doesn't seem to mind having the store in disarray, as he pulls people off stocking or reorganizing one section to start another section before the first one is finished. On a recent visit to the store in early November, I noticed a staff member working on the Christmas decoration section, with open boxes in the aisles as she put the light strings on the shelves. She then disappeared, leaving the boxes blocking the aisle. On the way to my car, I noticed her outside working on another area. When I mentioned this to my pal, he said this is common. Eric pulls people off one job to start another, even though the other job isn't as time-critical as the first.

Why does Eric do this? We don't know. We're guessing he really doesn't understand effective work flow of the store, and so he assigns people tasks as he thinks of them. He doesn't think ahead and prioritize, but just reacts as jobs occur to him.

My pal and others try to make suggestions for smoother work flow, but Eric doesn't implement them. We think he may be embarrassed that he doesn't know more, and taking someone else's suggestion would show his lack of experience. Or maybe he just thinks his way is the right way. But his store's sales figures are off, which he may blame on others.

Eric's biggest problem — which I've seen a lot — is over reliance on himself. If he were just to ask others for their input, he'd learn much better ways to approach the job flow. He doesn't have to take all the suggestions, but these people have been doing their jobs well for many more years than he's been around.

The questions to ask yourself, "Do I seek input from those who have more experience? Do I actively ask them, then listen to what they say without arguing? Then do I implement based on their suggestions?"

By not heeding others' wisdom and experience, you are not showing you are self-reliant. You're showing you're self-destructive.

About the Photo

In Ayutthaya, Thailand, Ava and I explored many ruins of temples in the ancient city. Some had been restored to their previous glory.

The details on these statues caught my eye, even though they were atop a building and not easy to see from the ground. I zoomed in to snap the photo, then cropped it closer to show the details.

Whenever I see ancient sculptures like these, I wonder about the artists and their process. How long did it take them to learn to chisel the stone? How many people worked on each figure? How long did it take them? Were they paid well? Did they come up with the design on their own, or did an architect design it?

Rarely do I get answers to these questions. Mostly, I'm left to appreciate the gifts they've left for the world to admire, centuries after their death.

Wouldn't it be great if we could all leave something of beauty for future generations to appreciate?

A fabulous adventure beckons you. Say yes to it.

©Rebecca Morgan, CSP, CMC
www.RebeccaMorgan.com

How can you apply this concept?

_____

_____

_____

_____

_____

Say "Yes" to Beckoning Adventures

I'm afraid of heights. Just thinking about climbing a ladder makes my stomach queasy.

So imagine my reaction when I was in Istanbul and a friend suggested I visit Cappadocia in central Turkey for a hot air balloon ride, I was not immediately excited.

That is an understatement.

The cautious side of me thought, "I'm traveling alone so no one to lean on if I get scared. It's not cheap at $300. I'd have to get up at 3:00 am for the hour's drive from my hotel. The balloons go high with no parachutes."

The adventurous side of me thought, "How cool! I've never been in a hot air balloon. It sails over a valley with unusual landscape. I'll be in the basket with others to talk to if I get scared. We'll watch the sunrise while aloft, and be back at the hotel by breakfast. I'll have the rest of the day to explore. They must have safety checks as they do this every day."

We have opportunities for adventures, yet few take them because of their cautious self-talk.

When pals hear that I go abroad several times a year, some say, "I wish I could afford that." I ask, "How much do you think it costs?" The response is usually, "I don't know." I ask, "Then how do you know you can't afford it?" When I tell them I commonly spend less than $500 for two to three weeks in Asia, they are stunned. I explain I use miles for air fare, and I find clean, safe, inexpensive lodging. They are agog.

They made a decision based on assumptions, not grounded information. Their fears, not facts, taint their thinking.

Adventures take some courage, requiring you to tamp down your fears to get in action.

I made a balloon ride reservation in Cappadocia.

It was chilly and dark when we arrived to see the balloons unfurled on the ground as they were filled. The dozen balloons near me slowly rose until vertical. Twenty riders climbed into our basket while our pilot briefed us on safety. Then we rose along with the sun.

> *Fears, not facts, taint our thinking*

Floating peacefully, I was awed by the dawn's evolving colors, witnessing nearly 100 brightly colored balloons rising nearly simultaneously. The quiet was pierced only by the occasional blast of a burner adding more air. The gondola's gentle sway was comforting as we ascended higher.

Rising to nearly 2000 feet, I inched toward the basket's center, away from the edge. It was too terrifying to look over the edge at the disappearing ground far below. However, when I looked straight out, I was mesmerized by dozens of colorful balloons dancing in the breeze against a snow-capped volcano in the distance. The flames from the burners contrasted with the sky. The chilly air on my face was invigorating.

Adventures may cause all your senses to heighten. Time slows as you notice what otherwise may have been overlooked. You see, smell, hear, feel and smell nuances. You feel fully alive.

When a fabulous adventure beckons you, say yes to it.

About the Photo

While our balloon was filling with air, other balloons were beginning to rise around us. These four surprised me when they peeked over a hill. I couldn't wait to begin my own adventure aloft.

The four compartments in the gondola were divided with five people each to evenly distribute the weight.

The two couples in my compartment knew each other and they were continually taking photos of each other as well as selfies. I was cowering in the middle near the pilot fearful to look over the edge.

Soon, though, I gathered my courage and asked one of the couples to trade with me so I could take photos over the edge. It was terrifying and exhilarating. My adrenaline rushed as we rose higher.

This experience is worth repeating as often as possible.

It can be interesting to understand the source of interpersonal conflict, but it's only useful if there's a lesson for you.

©Rebecca Morgan, CSP, CMC
www.RebeccaMorgan.com

How can you apply this concept?

_____

_____

_____

_____

Are You Difficult?

Have you ever been told you are difficult?

When I've labeled someone difficult, they have been some of these:

- ✦ Obstinate, uncooperative, inflexible, demanding, dictatorial.
- ✦ Undiplomatic, blunt, condescending, arrogant, caustic, hyper-critical, argumentative (often just for the sake of it, not because they believe their arguments).
- ✦ Incongruent, dishonest, passive-aggressive, uncommunicative, inconsiderate, insensitive, unreliable, defensive, petty.

So imagine my surprise to be told by a colleague, Peter, that Jim, whom I rarely work with, felt I was difficult.

While I am not fond of feedback from a third-party because specifics are minimal, if any, I take any negative feedback seriously. I use such feedback to explore how much, if any, of the feedback could be truthful, and how I can correct any dysfunctional behaviors.

It left me wondering what "difficult" really means.

Of course, "difficult" is subjective, so it's hard to know what another person's definition is. Because of reasons I don't want to get into, I did not feel I could ask Jim for clarification.

Since Peter could neither offer examples nor clarification, I reviewed my recent interactions with Jim to see if I could unearth what earned me the "difficult" moniker. In every recent interaction with Jim I could only remember being respectful, polite, friendly, acknowledging, professional, and clear.

We can, of course, have a skewed view of our behavior. I have increased my sensitivity to discern when I've offended someone or behaved inappropriately, and I apologize as soon as I realize it. Sometimes a friend brings to my attention some less-than-admirable behavior, and I am grateful for this immediate and direct feedback. I apologize as soon as possible.

If you've been told you are "difficult," do you wonder if this label is only about your behavior, or might it only minimally be about you? This "difficult" label made me explore if something else could be going on. Possibilities included:

- ✦ I'd been difficult with Jim, I just wasn't remembering when.
- ✦ Jim misheard or misinterpreted something I said/did but didn't clarify with me.

> *"Difficult" is subjective*

- ✦ I reminded Jim of someone with whom he has had problems.
- ✦ Jim was threatened by clear, confident, assertive people.
- ✦ Jim had trouble accepting the behaviors from a woman that he would have ignored from a man.
- ✦ Some of all of the above.
- ✦ Who knows?

While it can be interesting to understand the source of interpersonal conflict, it is not helpful unless there is a lesson for you.

I will be interacting with Jim in the future, and I will be as polite, professional, and friendly as I was before. Perhaps there will be an opening that will allow me to ask him directly about what I've done that is off-putting.

Have you been told you are difficult? How have you reacted?

About the Photo

Kayseri, the closest airport to Cappadocia, is a short plane ride from Istanbul.

Mert, a friend of a friend living in Kayseri, recommended the Sunak Cave Boutique Hotel, so I booked a room for three nights.

Hasan Dikici, the proprietor, picked me up in Kayseri, and we chatted, thanks to his broken English and my phone's English/Turkish translator.

I told him of my desire to take a hot-air balloon ride. He said he would arrange it.

At 3:30 a.m. I put on my warmest attire. It was chilly, even in June, and I'd read it was cold in the balloon once in the air.

After many stops to pick up others, our shuttle finally arrived at the launch site. It was still dark. There were dozens of balloons being filled, spread out over the valley.

I was fascinated watching the flames illuminate the inside of the balloons as they righted themselves with hot air. The fire was dramatic against the pre-dawn sky.

How can you apply this concept?

_____

_____

_____

_____

_____

Act on Your Curiosity

In the first chapter of *Give and Take*, by Adam Grant, he talks about Adam Rifkin, whom *Fortune* dubbed the Fortune Best Networker (he has more LinkedIn connections to the top 640 most powerful people on Fortune's lists). I decided to invite him to connect on LinkedIn.

Wanting to personalize my invitation to increase the likelihood he'd accept, I read his profile. He lives in Silicon Valley, 10 miles from me! He mentions he hosts a monthly meet up for start ups. I click on the link and discover the meet up is today in Palo Alto, 20 miles from me. I have the evening open, so I drive to the meet up.

Since there are 8600 people in his meet up group and dozens had RSVPed to the event, I thought I might just get to meet him and shake his hand.

I walked into the bar at the start time, and Adam and one other guy are there. I spent 30 minutes with Adam asking about his life, how being featured in the book has impacted his life, etc. I learned he was recently on Good Morning America to discuss his giving philosophy. We swapped notes about how big media hits can have no effect on our businesses. We brainstormed a project to create together.

I'm glad I acted on my curiosity. If nothing else, I added an interesting, big-hearted, humble, giving, man to my network.

Lessons for me:

- ✦ Act on reaching out, even if you think, "He would never accept my LinkedIn invitation. He must only hobnob with powerful people."
- ✦ Do some homework on the person. Had I sent a perfunctory

LinkedIn connection invitation I would not have learned about his meet up, the non-profit he supports and other details I could discuss with him. I knew to call him by his nickname.

✦ Arrive early. Few people are punctual, so I had an advantage by being the second guest to arrive and got to spend quality time with Adam.

✦ Be in the mindset of giving, not what you can ask for. I focused on helping him and never asked his input on my ventures. That might come later as we solidify our connection.

> *Do some homework before reaching out*

About the Photo

The 100 balloons in the sky that morning over Cappadocia was a spectacle to behold.

Our pilot deftly avoided colliding with other balloons. To do so could mean disaster, as the balloon skin could be torn by another balloon's basket.

We played leap frog with nearby balloons, seeing who could go higher faster. The pilots knew each other and called out to each other.

Soon we were soaring to our top altitude of 2000 feet. Mount Erciyes, a snow-capped dormant volcano near Kayseri, dominated the southern skyline.

It was magnificent.

All too soon, we descended to a field where our ground crew awaited with champagne and snacks. I wanted to go back up immediately.

How can you apply this concept?

_____

_____

_____

_____

_____

Your Conscientiousness Determines Your Success

Your level of conscientiousness has more effect on your life than you might have thought. It can determine many success factors, including your income, job satisfaction, health and even marital happiness.

If you have a high conscientiousness level and those around you don't, you'll experience a lot of frustration. You'll be continually faced with people who don't meet deadlines, honor their agreements, are inconsiderate of your and others' time, and have less commitment to quality output. I'm thinking "Big Five" personality traits test would be a helpful tool to ask potential employees (or mates!) to complete to know if you and they will be compatible.

The self-administered "Big Five" test assesses your conscientiousness level. It consists of fifty items you rate on how true they are about you on a five-point scale.

Conscientiousness is one of the "Big Five" — the others are agreeableness, extroversion, emotional stability (also called neuroticism), and intellect/imagination (also known as openness to experience). Each is important to one's success, but there's a tremendous amount of research linking conscientiousness with success in school and jobs — even higher income and job satisfaction.

University of Pennsylvania psychologist Angela Duckworth found conscientiousness traits to be more integral to children's scholarly success than IQ.

Those who test high in conscientiousness are shown to:

- get better grades in school and college
- commit fewer crimes

- stay married longer
- have more self control and stick-to-itiveness
- live longer

They tend to have
- high levels of thoughtfulness
- good impulse control
- goal-directed behaviors
- organizational skills
- consideration for others

They tend to:
- spend time preparing
- finish important tasks right away
- pay attention to details
- enjoy having a set schedule
- be punctual

Each of the Big Five characteristics has six sub-traits. For conscientiousness these are:
- self-efficacy (ability to accomplish tasks)
- orderliness (ability to organize)
- dutifulness (sense of duty and obligation)
- achievement-striving (commitment to achieving excellence)
- self-discipline (level of willpower)
- cautiousness (ability to think through possibilities before acting)

If you are not naturally conscientiousness you can learn to establish the habits to raise your conscientiousness. For example, if you are often late, you can learn to set an alarm on your phone or watch that alerts you of when to leave. If you tend to put off tasks, schedule them on your calendar so you're less likely to forget. Enlist the ideas of a highly conscientious person to share their thinking and tools for you to adopt.

About the Photo

My last evening in Cappadocia was perfectly spent at the Saruhan Caravanserai near Avanos, Turkey. Caravanserais are ancient dwellings built for those traveling along the Silk Road — precursors of hotels, and motels. Merchants frequented them since they were spaced in a day's trek intervals. They offered food, water, lodging, pens for the camels, and a safe place to store their wares during their rest.

My new friend, Hasan, proprietor of the Sunak Cave Boutique Hotel, drove me to the caravanserai for me to experience an authentic public viewing of the prayers by the Whirling Dervishes.

We arrived a little early so I explored the caravanserai. I imagined the hustle and bustle of this place when full of travelers and those who supplied them. Camels and other animals mixing with people. The smells of the camels, other animals and people, melding with the spices from cooking must have been pungent. The cacophony of music, conversation, and animals would be overwhelming.

But today it was nearly empty and quiet. I appreciated the peace.

The sun was low in the sky so the shadows were long. I was struck by the symmetry of these arched dividers separating several stalls where camels would have been kept. The shadows made it more dramatic.

"In Turkey, sharing a cup of coffee can last 40 years."
©Rebecca Morgan, CSP, CMC www.RebeccaMorgan.co

How can you apply this concept?

_____

_____

_____

_____

_____

A Cup Of Coffee Lasts 40 Years

In many countries it's common to be invited for a cup of coffee or tea as a way of extending hospitality. I hadn't fully understood the implications of this gesture until a recent speaking tour in Turkey.

I'd just given a 90-minute speech to 200+ members of the Eskisehir Chamber of Commerce. The Chamber president, Harun Karacan, a charming, successful businessman who spoke no English, invited me and my local host and friend, Tamer, to his office for coffee. His invitation was followed by this Turkish saying which his aide-de-camp, Arda, translated for me:

"In Turkey , a cup of coffee can last 40 years."

In other words, Arda explained, when we share a cup of coffee, we develop a relationship that can last for many decades.

I nodded showing my understanding.

There was only one problem.

I don't drink coffee. Nor tea.

I was in a prickly situation. I whispered to Tamer, "I don't drink coffee, but I'm guessing it would be rude to refuse a cup. So do you think I should just take a sip and pretend to drink it? I don't want to offend Mr. President."

Tamer nodded that I should just take a sip.

Mr. President, his entourage, Arda, Tamer and I arranged ourselves around his mammoth table. His attendants scurried in with coffee, along with individual silver candy dishes of nuts and Turkish delight (small cubes of chopped dates and nuts flavored with rosewater, dusted with sugar). We munched and chatted, with Arda at my side translating Mr. President's banter and my quips in return.

We discussed some of my presentation's key points and how Mr. President would implement them. Next time, we negotiated, he would provide a larger venue so the 200 more members who wanted to attend wouldn't be turned away.

> *Our bond grew as the coffee in the cup shrank*

Soon an aide handed Mr. President a small box. With some commentary, he presented it to me. It held a necklace, earrings and ring set with stone quarried only in Eskiehir. I thanked the president for his kindness. Earlier he'd given me a bag containing a plaque, another stone pendant, Turkish candy, and a sliver candy dish like the one before me now.

I could see now the impact of the Turkish saying. A cup of coffee does indeed make it possible for a long-lasting relationship. Our bond grew as the coffee in the cup shrank.

Lesson learned: Never refuse a cup of coffee again. You never know what kind of relationship can be forged between sips.

About the Photo

Above a village in Cappadocia, I came upon this tree outside a merchant's shop. Guess what he was selling? Yes. Nazars, also known as evil eyes. These talismans are believed to ward off evil.

Nazars are popular in the Mediterranean region. I've seen them on doors, hanging from windows, and embedded in entry ways. They are incorporated into jewelry designs and prayer beads. I was given a bracelet of nazars by an English-language teacher at a school where I spoke. I have a doorstop with a nazar. They ar purchased by locals and tourists alike.

This nazar-decorated tree transfixed me. The sun glinted off and through them. It seemed they were showing off their power. I'd never seen a sight like this.

I framed the shot to include the village and unusual rock formations in the background. Some of the buildings of this region are literally chiseled out of sandstone, thus aptly called cave dwellings.

Dependability is a superpower.

Strengthen yours.

©Rebecca Morgan, CSP, CMC
www.RebeccaMorgan.com

How can you apply this concept?

_____

_____

_____

_____

_____

Dependability Is a Superpower

- My contractor said he was coming to fix my dishwasher Thursday afternoon. He never arrived. Nor did he call or text he wasn't coming. So I waited.
- The salesperson said she would call at 10 am. She didn't. Nor did she email to alert me. So I waited.
- The client asked me to hold a date for a speech to her team. He said he'd get back to me by Friday. He didn't. I waited.

> *Stand out by delivering on your promises*

These are a few of the dozens of examples this year of people promising something then not following through.

Trying to give them some slack, I think, "They meant well." But did they? Or did they just say what they thought was appropriate in the moment? If they truly meant well, they'd do what they said they would.

When someone actually delivers on their promises, they stand out. It shows me we have the same values of integrity, dependability, and follow through. People who demonstrate these values receive my admiration.

Are people who don't demonstrate dependability flakes? Perhaps. Although they would never consider themselves so. When confronted, they will defensively sputter, "I'm just so busy." As if I'm not. Or, "It slipped my mind." You don't write down your commitments?

Or, "I'm at my kids'/boss's/mate's whim." So you have no say in how your time is spent? These excuses seem rather lame.

Maybe they didn't really want to do what was promised in the first place. They said they'd do it to be "nice." I don't think it's nice to lie to someone, and/or keep them waiting. That's downright rude.

Maybe they are concerned that if they say they can't do something, it will seem confrontational. Do they think it won't be even more confrontational when the person they've inconvenienced calls them on it? It will be more so.

If you make promises you don't keep, examine why. No matter your reasoning, start being more dependable. When you strengthen your dependability, you will be amazed how much more respect you receive, from others as well as yourself.

About the Photo

Five-year-old Luca greeted me in his Spiderman costume during my stay in Kayseri, Turkey. My host, Mert, lived in the same building as Luca's family.

Mert and I were invited by Luca's family to iftar, the fast-breaking meal eaten after sunset every day during Ramadan.. For many families it is a feast. It was no different with Luca's family.

Luca's mother and grandmother had already set the table with some food when we arrived. Luca greeted me in his Spiderman costume. We watched the clock on the TV counting down the minutes before the fast was officially broken. At the right moment, we were invited to sit at the table to begin our dinner.

Neither Luca nor his grandparents spoke English, with the help of Mert and Luca's mother,, we made ourselves understood. I appreciated their kindness in inviting this stranger to share a special meal with them.

One of my delights in travel is experiencing the kindness of locals. It would be hard for me to be invited to something like this if I were just a tourist.

I've attended weddings in Cambodia and the Philippines even though I didn't know the couple. I was invited to tea at the home of a beauty shop owner after she did my hair. I accompanied a friend to a champagne tasting event at a wine merchant's home in Cambodia. A client invited me to her home for snacks in Brunei. Another made me the guest of honor at dinner in her home in Singapore, even though I'd only met her once.

I love experiencing how locals live. Luca is part of a great memory.

Stop offering 'feedback.' Share 'refinements.'

How can you apply this concept?

_____

_____

_____

_____

_____

Stop Offering Feedback

I'm sure I'm not the only one who bristles when someone asks, "Can I give you some feedback?" It's usually unsolicited advice about something the giver feels you did wrong. Rarely is there any inquiry first into your reasoning for the behavior, just, in essence, "You did something I don't like." It is often focused on what you have already done, feeling like criticism for something you now cannot change, rather than suggestions for moving forward.

Some feedback is completely unhelpful. When someone writes a generality on a presentation evaluation, or passes on a third-party opinion, there's no way to ask questions for clarification on what was offensive and how you could make it less so.

> *Some feedback is completely unhelpful*

My colleague, John B. Molidor, Ph.D., professor of psychiatry with a focus on neuroscience and psychology, recently shared with me that when we hear "feedback" the part of the brain that activates is associated with flight or fight. Thus, we shut down our receptivity to what comes next, and get defensive.

Should we eschew receiving all suggestions to improve our behavior? Of course not. It's valuable to hear someone we trust's perspective and ideas for polishing our actions.

When someone offers you feedback, immediately ask, "What would work better for you next time?" It focuses the giver on the future, not the past, and you can then decide if their suggestion would work for you or not.

If you don't relish "feedback" from unskilled givers, yet find yourself compelled to offer a tweak to someone's behavior, try offering a "refinement" instead of "feedback." You may think this is an unnecessary change in wording that means essentially the same thing, but "refinement" doesn't come with the same emotional charge as "feedback". Some may think this is being too sensitive, that the end result is the same — hearing someone's reaction to your behavior. "Refinement" connotes future behavior, not criticizing unchangeable, past behavior.

I believe the initial phrasing of the offer has a lot to do with how the information is received. When someone offers a refinement, I interpret the offer as "Most everything was fine, but here's a tiny area for polishing." I think most of us would welcome this.

About the Photo

The warm June day enticed me to lunch at an outside cafe in Istanbul. From the second story patio, I had a perfect view of Hagia Sophia, which is now a museum.

I love people watching. My perch afforded me a bird's-eye view of throngs of tourists crisscrossing the plaza below. Buses discharged visitors there. I watched as their tour guides marched them toward the museum.

This entertained me through my lunch of Turkish salad (the same as Greek salad, but don't ever call it that in Turkey). I lingered as the scene was too engrossing to leave. I busied myself looking for signs to discern the visitors' countries of origin.

Before finally leaving, I wanted to memorialize my delightful lunch break, so I raised my camera to take a few shots. The sunlight was so bright I couldn't see clearly what I was snapping. Only when back at my inn did I see I'd caught a bird, mid-flight, with its wings outstretched. Perfect!

It was not my photography prowess that captured this shot. Instead, it was all the bird's timing. I am grateful.

Eschew frivolous talk.
Seek meaningful conversation instead.

©Rebecca Morgan, CSP, CMC
www.RebeccaMorgan.com

How can you apply this concept?

_____
_____
_____
_____
_____

Eschew Frivolous Talk. Seek Meaningful Conversation

Frivolous: unworthy of serious attention; trivial; of little value.

"And then he said...then she said...and then...and then..." and on and on.

Have you been on the listening end of frivolous talk? You know it when you hear it — when someone prattles on and on about people you don't know, will never meet, and don't care about. Or when someone keeps talking and talking, saying little, perhaps even repeating themselves. A friend has a saying for this: "I'm just talking here — not saying anything."

Have you found yourself spending time involved in — or listening to — more frivolous talk than you'd care to? I know I have. But I

> *"I'm just talking here — not saying anything."*

also had an experience that made me realize how much I contribute to frivolous talk.

At a multiple-day off-site personal growth workshop, we'd been told that this workshop could be life-changing if we followed the guidance of our facilitators 100% while we were there. I trusted these leaders, so I did the exercises fully.

The first day we were told there was to be no frivolous talk. In fact, there was to be no talk at all outside of our workshop room, other than to discuss logistics issues (e.g., car pooling). In other words, we were to be silent.

I was struck by how many times I'd think about chatting with my classmates about unimportant things—the weather, her pretty jacket, could he pass the salt. I saw how much "noise" I contributed. These things weren't really important, or I didn't need to speak to communicate them.

By forcing us into silence, we saw how little of our usual babble really needs to be said. When the silence was lifted a few days later, we were much quieter than we'd been before. When we did speak, it was to ask a deeper question, or to share a meaningful insight.

Although I've drifted back into some chatter, I talk less now than before.

Why don't you try it? You don't have to be silent, but think about what you say before you say it. Ask yourself "Does this really need to be said? Will it make a difference to my listener?" If not, then button it up!

About the Photo

The ancient city of Bagan, Myanmar (formerly Burma) is famous for its 2,200 temples. After appreciating the beauty of a few of them, I decided the best way to see them from a new perspective was from a hot air balloon.

Three of my traveling buddies and I were picked up well before dawn. Our destination was a large field where the balloon operators were filling the unfurled balloons with hot air. We watched, fascinated, as the giant balloons slowly rose.

Soon we climbed into the basket along with four strangers. Within minutes we were aloft, barely skirting tree tops. We shared the sky with 18 other balloons.

Roosters crowed in the distance breaking the silence. We were startled by roar of the burners adding more air to take us higher. In between bursts, it was peacefully quiet.

As the sun crept to the horizon, the sky subtly changed its palette. Soon it was blazing orange, encircling the first temples to come into sight with an orange cast.

Our view from aloft, coupled with the stunning sunrise, was breathtaking. We looked down directly on top of the ancient temples, giving us a totally new perspective.

If you're ever in Myanmar, don't miss Bagan. Ideally, you'll be in a hot air balloon at sunrise.

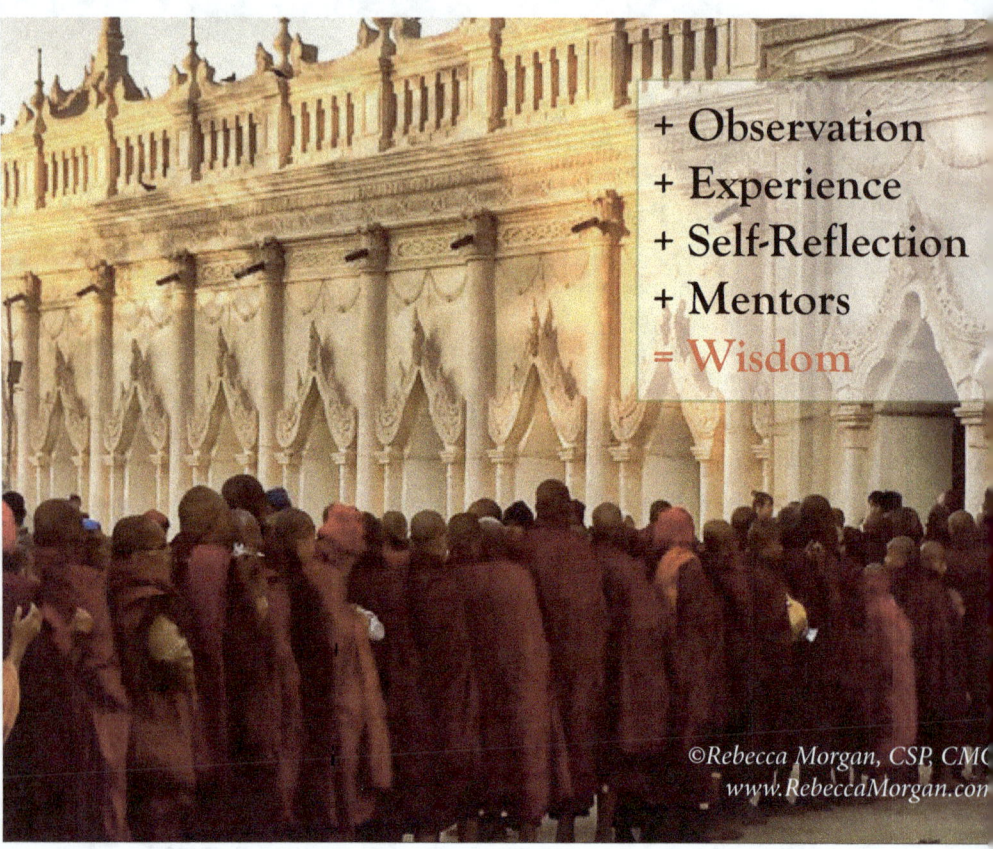

How can you apply this concept?

_____
_____
_____
_____
_____

The Path to Wisdom

I work closely with a tech company which isn't a client. They have thousands of employees around the world. Their headquarters alone houses a few thousand employees.

Because I am a super user of their site, I am invited to participate in special programs — some beta tests, some educating new, seasoned and prospective users. The few dozen staff with whom I've worked are smart.

However, because these intelligent people don't have a lot of work experience, I find they make decisions that aren't wise. They don't think through the repercussions on their users before enacting changes. They don't decide actions based on long-term ramifications, nor on the message their decision sends about the company's values.

I find they lack wisdom.

They have some seasoned bosses, but not that many. And the ones with more experience seem to have so many people reporting to them that no one gets the kind of guidance they should.

It made me ponder how someone gains wisdom. I narrowed it down to three things: experience, observing what works and what doesn't, and mentors.

Let's take each of these in turn.

Experience

> Some say you learn best from your own mistakes. If you are smart and introspective, after each failure you ask yourself some important questions. Starting with, "What could I have done to create a different outcome?" You don't blame the failure on

everyone but yourself. Others may have contributed to it, but you did too. The more you are willing to look at your contribution, the better able you'll be to head off failure in a similar situation in the future.

Companies now ask job applicants about their failures and their lessons from them. The thinking is that if you haven't failed, you haven't taken a risk. And if you haven't learned something from those experiences, you aren't emotionally mature enough to be a good team member.

That's not to say you can't also learn from successes. The key is to be astute and notice what you did to create the success so you can repeat it consciously. Some people think they are naturally successful without having to plan to be that way. They are not aware of what they've done to be successful so it will be harder for them to repeat the behaviors.

Observation

Wise and successful people are keen observers. They learn not only from their own successes and failures, but from others. They notice what others do and the outcomes of those actions. They vow not to repeat the mistakes they watch others make. And they decide to adapt successful behaviors.

Perceptive observation includes curiosity. You want to ask, "I wonder what outcome he intended to have when he berated that employee." "I'm curious to understand his motivation for not telling anyone the team goals had changed." "I'd be fascinated to know what he was thinking when he said she was a pain in the neck during the public acknowledgement of her."

It's easy to judge the offending behavior as bad and wrong when it is different from what you would do or like. Yet different people have different motivations as well as skills. By observing their behavior with curiosity you may uncover an understanding of someone's motivations that doesn't match your own.

Mentors

An effective mentor is someone who takes interest in helping you succeed by offering guidance, input and candid feedback. If she thinks you are doing something stupid, she tells you in a way you can hear. A mentor can be short-term and offer input on a finite project, or long-term, helping you mold your career and life.

A mentor can provide a higher-level, long-term view of your actions. He can help you see the messages you're sending by your actions and decisions. He can assist you in seeing the broader ramifications of your behavior.

When I've been hired to be an executive coach, the relationship is that of a mentor. I can see beyond the issues at hand and help the person by asking probing questions. Ideally, a coach or mentor doesn't tell you what to do, but asks you questions which help you make wiser decisions.

How will you help make your people wiser?

Can you enlist any of the above to increase your own wisdom?

About the Photo

At dawn, we arrived at a nearby temple for Bagan's (in Myanmar) monthly Full-Moon Festival. Monks of all ages lined up outside to receive gifts of rice, sweets, fruit, other food and money from villagers, some of whom traveled many hours.

The contrast of their burgundy robes against the cream temple walls was stunning in the morning light. I couldn't stop taking photos.

Be a conscious conversationalist.

©Rebecca Morgan, CSP, CMC www.RebeccaMorgan.com

How can you apply this concept?

_____

_____

_____

_____

_____

Be a Conscious Conversationalist

Being a conscious conversationalist is critical to a long-term relationship, whether with a coworker, customer, or friend—at least for me. I've encountered many people who are conversationally challenged. Since it is doubtful your friends or colleagues will volunteer that you are an inept conversationalist, as a public service I thought I'd delineate some of the most common conversational culprits.

- **Taking most of the airtime.** A conscious conversationalist will be aware of approximately how much of the talk time she is taking and when it begins to feel like she's monopolized the conversation, turn the focus on the other person. You can simply say, "I've been talking non stop. Tell me (something relevant to them)."

- **Repeating yourself.** If you aren't paying enough attention to what you are saying that you repeat yourself, how much do you think the other person will feel you're listening to them?

- **Turning the focus back to you.** I had a recent conversation with someone I'd just met. He regularly turned the conversation to himself. We were talking about the world's awareness of US affairs. Since I hadn't shared much by this point, I said "When I was in Malaysia last summer, I was amazed at how many of my contacts watched the Democratic convention on CNN." His next line was not, "What did you make of that?" or "What did they think of US politics?" or "What were you doing in Malaysia?" No. It was, "A friend has a manufacturing plant in Malaysia that makes dolls. He wants to hire me to do some work for him. Look it up at www.xxx.com."

- **Not asking relevant follow-up questions.** This same caller said he thought I was fascinating. Which I found odd because I had said barely 10 sentences after 30 minutes into the call. He could have found out about me by asking relevant follow-up questions to my comments, as I illustrated above. If both parties merely jump into a conversation with their own stories or thoughts, it's as if two people are having sequential monologues. To really get to know someone's thoughts, values, and opinions, you have to dig deeper into what they share.

✦ **Delving into unimportant details.** Your conversation partner doesn't need to know every detail of your story. Try to keep it pithy but still include relevant information. Most people could cut their chatter by half, if not 2/3, if they focused on just key elements to get their thought across. If someone wants more detail they'll ask. Better to error on the side of pithiness.

✦ **Interrupting.** When someone is talking, let them finish their story or thought. Of course, this is a challenge if they are going on and on and on about something of no interest to you. If you need to interrupt to clarify something, do so with, "I need to interrupt before you go on because I'm confused about..." You are interrupting to better understand what they are sharing, not to change the subject or focus the conversation back on you.

✦ **Not letting the other person answer your questions.** If you ask a question and as soon as your conversation partner starts sharing, you interject, "That happened to me, too! Let me tell you about it..." you are showing you don't really care to know about them.

✦ **Too many non sequiturs.** If you can't stay with the thread of the conversation and are continually changing the subject (often back to focusing on you), it is difficult to have an in-depth discussion. Yes, we all get reminded of something that is a little off the subject, and if you find your stream of consciousness takes you far afield, you can acknowledge that, "This is a tad off topic, but your comment reminded me of...." Or if you have more to share on the topic but your partner has gone on a tangent, simply say, "I had another thought I wanted to share on ...."

Avoid common conversational culprits

✦ **Short or curt answers.** While I believe in being pithy, curt or short answers are not attractive. If you don't want to talk about something, simply say, "I'd rather not go there right now." or "I'll tell you about that after we've gotten to know each other a bit better."

✦ **Being unaware of what might be of interest to the listener.** If you babble on about things that your listener probably doesn't care about, then they lose interest not only in the conversation, but with developing a relationship with you. If your side of the dialog is filled with information about your children, grandchildren, first job, high school, your friends (and your friends' children and grandchildren), you'll soon lose your listener.

✦ **Try to edit in your mind before spewing out whatever crosses your thoughts.** Think, "Would this likely interest my listener?" and delete anything that you can't say yes to, no matter how much interest it holds for you. Once someone knows and cares about you, they are more interested in the broader spectrum of your life. But not at first.

- **Boasting.** If you are the hero of every story, it gets tedious to listen to you. If you are proud of something, you can start off with, "I'm so excited..." But to keep interjecting stories where you are the champion will earn you the title of bore.
- **Name dropping incessantly.** This same caller told me how he had put up a Facebook page and a bunch of politicians had asked to be his friend. He named the politicians, none of whom I recognized. If you have to name drop regularly to show how important you are, you're really telegraphing your insecurities.

We all have some poor conversational habits, myself included. The key is to get some honest feedback from those who care about you. Ask them to be candid with you. Show them the above list and ask if you are guilty of any of the items. And engage them to help you increase your awareness by saying something like "TMI (too much information)" if you start to go into unimportant details.

This will yield not only stronger friendships, but more solid relationships with colleagues and customers.

About the Photo

Three gal pals and I visited Paris a few days before attending a conference there. Two of our group had never been to Paris before so we sought some classic sight-seeing experiences.

Heading out on a beautiful sunny November day, we visited Notre Dame, then took in a Seine River cruise. I loved seeing the sights from the river. The bridges all had their own personality, with different architecture and statuary.

When our boat floated by Notre Dame, the view of the South Rose Window was an uncommon one. I caught the flowers from the boat in the frame and snapped away.

Humor, at someone else's expense, can cut more deeply than you'll ever know.

©Rebecca Morgan, CSP, CMC
www.RebeccaMorgan.com

How can you apply this concept?

_____

_____

_____

_____

_____

Humor, at Someone Else's Expense, Can Cut More Deeply Than You'll Ever Know

In my family caustic teasing was de rigueur. We would be teased about anything the teaser thought was funny, no matter how humiliating, and with no thought to how it would leave the receiver feeling. Didn't do well on a test? You'd be teased about being dumb. Boyfriend broke up with you? He must have finally figured out you are a loser. Lose the student election? They could see you are a follower, not a leader.

The more humiliating the better, from the teaser's perspective. This wasn't limited to us kids teasing each other; our parents joined in — or initiated — with glee. The more sensitive the receiver was about the topic, the more the tormentor enjoyed it.

Have you ever teased others about something you knew they were sensitive?

It's a form of bullying.

In my mind teasing — really it was put downs — was normal, so I teased people indiscriminately — friends, family, my then-husband, strangers. It went over better with some than others. My then-husband would laugh at my zingers targeting him. When friends witnessed this, they thought I was mean. Which I was. But I didn't really comprehend this because he would laugh. I had been raised that this was a way to show affection, even though it often stung when I was on the receiving end. Now I know this is twisted.

I had become a female Don Rickles. I was a human Triumph the Insult Comic Dog. If someone laughed I thought it was fine.

As I grew more aware, I saw that this was really a power play. Family members would tease each other to assert dominance until the one being teased would cry or storm out slamming doors. The exchange still hurt even if it was I who "won."

I now see humor at another's expense (teasing, put downs, "funny" insults, digs or zingers) as abuse. There are many forms of abuse, including verbal and emotional.

You know you're bullying when the other person doesn't take it well and you hear yourself saying, "What, you can't take a joke?" or "You're too sensitive — I was joking." or "Lighten up — I was just kidding!" Joking by making fun of someone else is passive-aggressive bullying.

In fact, you may be saying this now: "You're being too sensitive. Joking around is fun! My friends tweak each other all the time. We laugh about it!" They may laugh because if they didn't it would make them seem weak. However, it may hurt deeply. I've heard people tease pals about their weight, balding, income, looks, intelligence, and relationships (or lack thereof). The problem is that teasing is often based on a kernel of truth. The receiver may not be self-conscious about it, or he may be very sensitive. You never know.

Even if the person laughs, when she is alone, she may have serious self-doubts about the thing you've pointed out with your cutting humor. The teasing may cause her to go into a self-loathing spiral. She may self-harm as a way to cope.

Some people think, "I have to zing back to show I'm not weak." You can be strong without resorting to bullying. You don't want to lower yourself to the other's level.

Teasing has cost me relationships. Thanks to caring friends and professionals pointing out how my teasing is not conducive to healthy relationships, I've become more aware of this habit and I've curtailed it significantly. Is it totally gone? I have to admit I sometimes find myself spewing a zinger. But it is rare now. When I do, I apologize to the person afterwards.

When you find yourself engaging in teasing and zingers, ask yourself what you think it accomplishes. If you think that's just how you interact with your friends, try not contributing and see what happens. Do you feel you are closer or less? My guess is the former. Your friends might actually start zinging you for your lack of zinging!

If teasing, digs and zings are part of your friends' and family's behavior, try this: zing yourself. Make yourself the focus of the dig. Be the butt of the joke. They may pile on. But at least you're not inflicting harm onto others.

About the Photo

Our group was invited on a sunset dinner cruise on the Mekong River, between Thailand and Laos. I'm always a sucker for sunsets, cruises and dinner.

After dinner, the sun began to set. The boat was traveling east, so I went to the back to watch the sun set unimpeded by the boat's structure.

The wake made beautiful textures in the water, which amplified the setting sun's colors. I was transfixed.

I took shot after shot of the evolving image. Soon, several of my fellow amateur-photographer friends joined me on the back steps leading to the water. They became as enamored of the spectacle as I was.

Darkness was approaching fast. We knew our opportunity to catch this beauty was fleeting. We did our best to capture what we saw.

Time-conscious communicators share only listener-relevant information.

©Rebecca Morgan, CSP, CMC
www.RebeccaMorgan.com

How can you apply this concept?

_____
_____
_____
_____
_____

Become A Time-Conscious Communicator

I've noticed a lot of people — maybe 90% — aren't very conscious of their conversational habits. The most common habit I've noticed is no awareness of the relevance of what the speaker is saying to their conversational partner.

I began to wonder how much more productive we would be if we focused our comments on only those of importance to our listeners. Granted, we can't always know what the other would find important, and sometimes, with close friends and family, we want to share something that is significant to us as a way of sharing ourselves, but may only be interesting to our loved one because they care about us.

But let's focus on workplace conversations.

Have you been caught in a conversation with a co-worker that has taken way more time than it needed because the co-worker rambled on and on? I'd be surprised if you said "no" as this is common. Imagine how much more you could both get done if the conversation stayed focused on salient information.

I recently had discussions with two doctors treating me and was astounded at how much time they wasted on irrelevant information. Doctors' time is typically rationed carefully, often with only 15 minutes allotted per patient. So you'd think they would be hyper-aware of their wasting time sharing info that has no bearing on that patient. But many of them are not.

One doctor had asked me to watch a video explaining a procedure she recommended. When we next talked, I began by saying I'd watched the video. She then spent five minutes telling me what was in the video. She didn't ask if I had questions about the video; she just launched into explaining what I already knew, adding information that wasn't relevant to my situation. She wasted $^1/_3$ - $^2/_3$ of our time on irrelevant information.

Another doctor spent five of our 15 minutes telling me the history of the drug she was prescribing, and its warnings for pregnant women. She could see by my chart that was not relevant to my situation, nor was it germane to understand the history of the meds. She could have used our time more wisely, or we could have ended early, which we both would have been happy about.

> *Give only enough information to be useful to your listener*

The key to being a time-conscious communicator is to give only enough information to be useful to your listener. A few sentences will usually suffice. You don't want to be curt, but you also don't want to ramble. If your listener needs more information, s/he will nearly always ask. Then you can elaborate.

So before going on and on and on, ask your listener if s/he has questions or wants more detail. My guess is most will be just fine with an overview.

About the Photo

At the end of a two-week trip to India, our group leader suggested visiting the Jagmandir Island Palace, on Pichola Lake in Udaipur.

The late-afternoon boat ride provided a refreshing respite from the heat. Even in January, the weather can be oppressive for those not accustomed to it.

After encircling the lake, we docked at the palace. With water taxis coming frequently, we decided the waterfront bar was the best place to enjoy the sunset.

While I waited for the sun to put on its show, I explored the public areas of the palace. From atop an outcrop, I loved this view of the elephant statues greeting visitors.

The cool breeze from the lake — coupled with cocktails — made this the perfect place to enjoy our last night in Udaipur.

Venting is toxic. Don't infect others.

How can you apply this concept?

_____

_____

_____

_____

_____

Venting Is Toxic

"I need to vent" is an oft-heard expression when one is frustrated.

Great that the person is clear on what they need.

However, they often vent indiscriminately to whomever is within earshot. Strangers have expressed their frustration to me, even when the cause of their angst had nothing to do with me.

Venters say it makes them feel better to get their upset off their chest. I think of it like coughing without covering your mouth — it makes you feel better to release what needs to be released, but you are spreading your negative thoughts to those around you, most of whom don't want to hear it. So while it may make *you* feel better, it makes other innocent bystanders feel worse.

You are spreading your bad vibes to others who may be inflicted. They may be having a perfectly fine day until you dump your vexation onto his/her head. Some may slough it off, but others will allow it to taint their mood. Do you really want to do that — leave bad emotions in your wake?

So what to do if you find it useful to express your frustration to others? Here are some options:

Don't express it to anyone. Try writing it out. Then toss it. Why would you hang on to it?

Walk around the block or go into your car and vent. Mutter whatever you would have said to another person. If you're walking don't worry that others will think you've gone off the deep end. They may have already thought that.

Enlist *one* confidant to be your Vent Buddy. You both agree you will allow the other person to vent *one* time day for *one minute*. That's right — only one minute. Your Vent Buddy will time you and tell you when to shut up. The Vent Buddy will not offer advice, but will merely listen.

The only times I believe it is appropriate to vent to more than your Vent Buddy is when there is something to share that will likely be of benefit to the listener, or when you are seeking input on how to handle the situation better next time. So vent only when you have something to learn or to share.

If a customer complained about something you or your organization can do differently, share the info with coworkers to see if your organization can make the change.

If your colleague was curt to you and you know she is caring for a terminally ill loved one, you can share with other colleagues to treat her especially kindly, even when she is grumpy.

If you lost your temper at a fellow parent during your kids' game, you can ask your pals for input on how to deal more respectfully to him next time.

I learned in a personal development course years ago that one should only complain to someone who can do something about it. That had a major impact on me and now I complain much less. Instead of a complaint, I try to seek a lesson if I can't find someone who can do something about it.

How can you shift your venting to make it less toxic and more productive?

> *You feel better, but others feel worse*

About the Photo

My pal Karleen called with a proposition. The gal pal with whom she'd planned to spend a week in Bali had to cancel with two week's notice. She asked, "Would you be available? Your lodging would be covered as my friend can't get a refund."

My passport is always up to date, my client appointments were flexible, so of course I said yes.

We stayed in Ubud, in the cool mountains, about an hour's drive from the beach and airport. Our guesthouse was a 5-minute walk from the hustle and bustle of downtown. It was close enough to be convenient, yet far enough to avoid the noise.

Exploring the sights of Ubud led us to a museum with this marvelous, moss-covered sculpture. I liked the feeling of tranquility emitted by the stature, even though it looks like we may have disturbed her from her slumber, since she is clutching a her blanket. With her head propped up, she seems nonchalant, as if saying, "Well, since you woke me up, let's have a chat."

An advantage of travel is experiencing art you'd never encounter at home. Plus, you get to be creative making up the circumstances around pieces like this one.

It doesn't take long to feel connected with someone.

You can touch each other's hearts with a smile, an eye connection, and a little conversation.

©Rebecca Morgan, CSP, CMC
www.RebeccaMorgan.com

How can you apply this concept?

_____

_____

_____

_____

_____

Eight Lessons Learned from a Bali Girls Home

It's trite to say that you better appreciate what you have when you see others who have less.

It's hackneyed to say you've received more than you gave when you give to those who have less than you.

It's condescending to believe that those who have fewer material goods are less well off than you.

So instead, let me focus on the unexpected lessons I learned from a visit to a Bali girls' group home.

When I accepted the invitation from my friend Karleen to accompany her for a week-long vacation to Bali, I hadn't realized the group home visit was part of the deal. When she told me she'd like to see the girls she'd met there two years previously, I immediately said I wanted to go with her. I'd heard about this group home, the Widhya Asih #4, from two other friends who support it through Together We Can Change the World.

"Number 4" is unusual in that it houses 70 teenage girls. Prior to our trip, I asked the group home manager, Tina, what the girls needed. The list included umbrellas, toothbrushes, toothpaste, and "girly" items — hair ornaments, lotions, shampoo, nail polish, etc.

Knowing my neighbors like contributing to others, I emailed them the wish list. Soon I received donations of new age-appropriate clothing, as well as 70 sets of handmade jewelry. These gifts were from some neighbors I'd never met. Wow!

> Lesson 1: When you ask for a good reason, people will blow you away with what they contribute.

I connected with a colleague in Bali whom I'd never met. When he heard of our wanting to visit Number 4, he immediately offered transportation, as it was an hour away from where we were staying. His wife and brother-in-law were our drivers/guides.

> Lesson 2: Sometimes just sharing your plans evokes offers of help from others.

We'd told Tina our planned arrival time, so when we pulled up a bevy of girls greeted us with huge smiles and friendly attitudes. They seemed excited to have visitors and treated us like celebrities.

They politely introduced themselves, shaking our hands and asking our names. They had no trouble with "Rebecca" but "Karleen" was an uncommon name for them to remember. I illustrated it for them by saying "car" and placing my hands on an imaginary steering wheel, then leaned to the right — with my hands still on the non-existent wheel — as I said "lean." They giggled and imitated me.

> Lesson 3: People will respond positively if you make it easy for them to remember unusual words.

Touring the facilities, we viewed their sewing room where they make items to sell through a US retail outlet. They supplement the group home's revenue which enables more girls to attend school and have what they need to survive.

When asked to see their bedroom, several friendly girls revealed a neat, clean room the size of many Americans' walk-in closet with 2 sets of bunk beds for 4 girls. A window looked out on a courtyard. Four stacking lockers stored each girl's worldly belongings. I realized they didn't react as I'd imagine some American kids would — embarrassed at how little they had — but instead they were proud of their room's order.

> Lesson 4: Sometimes we forget how few possessions it would take for us to be happy.

We gathered the girls in a large semi-circle to distribute the gifts from our jam-packed suitcases. We unpacked the clothes, shampoo, toothbrushes, lotions, and other goodies. Tina explained that each girl would choose one item until everyone had something, then they would choose a second item. Some of the girls were busy doing chores so we saved some items to let them have a pick of treats.

My generous neighbor had donated teen items like jeans, t-shirts with rhinestones, sequined hats, cute tops, skirts and one special party dress. I was sure these would be the most coveted items.

> *We forget how few possessions it would take for us to be happy*

At home while packing, I looked around for new items in my house that I thought might be useful to the girls. I'd bought some ankle socks in various colors that were still in the package, so threw them in. I separated each color so the girls could choose among the pink, purple and gray socks. To my amazement, a girl rushed to pick the gray pair when Tina told them to pick!

> Lesson 5: What may seem a top prize to you will be eschewed in favor of a lesser (to you) item, but will be a treasure to another. I'd never have guessed a pair of gray anklets would be valued over cute, fashionable tops and jeans.

The girl who chose the black party dress told others who also had admired it they could borrow it for special events when she wasn't using it.

> Lesson 6: Some might think that having nearly no special belongings would cause one to be stingy and possessive. This girl showed that even though dressy clothes were rare in this environment, she could still be generous with her treasure.

The girls seemed appreciative of all our gifts, even toothbrushes, toothpaste, and dental floss! Sometimes we undervalue utilitarian items thinking only fun gifts will be appreciated. But these girls seemed thrilled with everything we brought.

> Lesson 7: If you receive a gift that is more useful than fun, know that if you didn't have the useful one it would make your life less comfortable. If you didn't get a new toothbrush very often, receiving one is valued.

We hadn't been there much more than an hour, but we'd had some sweet interactions with a number of the girls. We'd wished we could stay longer, but our driving hosts had a previous engagement. As we began our goodbyes, girls wanted their pictures taken with us and asked for our Facebook names so they could friend us.

> Lesson 8: It doesn't take long to feel connected with someone. If you are both authentic and open, you can touch each other's hearts with a smile, an eye connection, and a little conversation.

My biggest lesson was to cement my philosophy to say "yes" to opportunities to help others when I can. It really does enrich our lives more than we could have possibly imagined.

Say "yes" to opportunities to help others

About the Photo

Karleen and I decided we'd like to see a bit of Bali's countryside so we hired Wayan to show us. My friend Holly had recommended him. Unbeknownst to us, he was the owner of a local resort who liked to take visitors to his favorite back-country haunts.

We met Wayan before dawn so we could watch the sky change colors in the countryside. When we came into a small village, the locals scrutinized us — we imagined they thought, "What are these foreigners doing so far from the tourist area? What do they want?" We immediately smiled and waved. Their skepticism vanished and they return the smiles and waves.

Wayan is famous in these parts of Bali. If the villagers saw him first, their faces lit up with smiles as they waved. He'd slow down to greet them as we passed.

The bright green color of the rice paddies was striking. In this picture, you can see by the light it is morning. The villagers were typically in the fields, planting, weeding, harvesting, and tending to their crop. Occasionally, we'd see water buffalo in the fields, sometimes yoked to plow.

Wayan explained that most village houses are built in compounds so family can live close to each other. He said all the villagers take care of each other, even if they aren't related. If someone is sick, others bring food. If a child needs to be looked after, others will do it. If you need help, often others show up before you ask.

At the end of the four hours, Wayan took us back to his resort for breakfast. He wanted to make sure we did not go hungry. He was extending the local caring to us, too.

How can you apply this concept?

_____

_____

_____

_____

_____

Don't Make Decisions for Me Without Consulting Me

It happens at work:

"She too busy to be on the committee."

"He wouldn't like this new project. He likes what he's doing now."

"He has a family at home so won't want to take the trip to visit the new customer."

"She doesn't like public speaking so we shouldn't ask her to speak at the conference."

It happens in one's personal life:

"He won't want to accompany me to the class/concert/play."

"She's fussy about eating so we she won't want to join us to try the new restaurant."

"He's not a big outdoors buff so we shouldn't bother inviting him to join our hike."

"She doesn't like crowds so we won't ask her to come to the parade."

While we think we are doing the person a favor by not involving him/her in our plans, we are making a decision for her without consulting her. We think we know her well enough to know what she would like.

However, he might have changed his mind about what you think he wouldn't like. Or he might have decided it is time to try that activity again. Or she may have had an awakening that has motivated her to stretch her concepts of what she likes and doesn't like.

So while you think you are being thoughtful, you're actually not. It is more thoughtful to involve the person and let her make the decision for herself. That is the most thoughtful act.

She may say, "You're right. I don't like skiing. But I do like relaxing in front of the fire with a good book in the lodge while the snow is falling. So I'll come with you to the mountains, and enjoy myself in the lodge while you ski. I'll then whip up a delicious meal for us to enjoy when you're done on the slopes." If you had not asked her to come on the trip, you would have missed out on her company and would have prevented her from having an enjoyable outing.

At work, when you decide someone would not like a new assignment, you are preventing him from taking on a new task to stretch his skills and experience. Just because he's declined in the past doesn't mean he'll say no this time. People change. Don't assume you know the response this time. Allow the person to determine their response now. It doesn't mean if they say yes they will do the same in the future.

When someone has previously declined an invitation, I'll ask like this, "I know in the past you've said you aren't interested in traveling because of your family obligations. I don't want to assume that is still the case, so wanted to give you the opportunity to decide about this upcoming trip. If you say no, that is fine, I'll keep asking you each time and let you make the decision."

This is much more respectful than making the decision for the person based on their past preferences. Wouldn't you appreciate being asked and allowed to make a decision on what's best for you now, not what you decided in the past?

About the Photo

Visiting Seville, Spain in November was a perfect time. The pleasant temperature during the day, required only a light jacket or sweater in the evening.

None of the four of us women traveling buddies had researched what to do in the city. We were lucky to have met Pepe the previous week in Paris who lived in Seville and offered to show us the sights.

Pepe's English was perfect. His flexible schedule allowed him to take us for a bike ride along the river, to a tapas dinner, and other sights around town. When he couldn't accompany us, he made suggestions, like visiting The Real Alcázar, a medieval palace a block from our rental home.

The palace was ornate, both inside and out. I was struck by the colors and patterns of the Patio de las Doncellas courtyard pictured here.

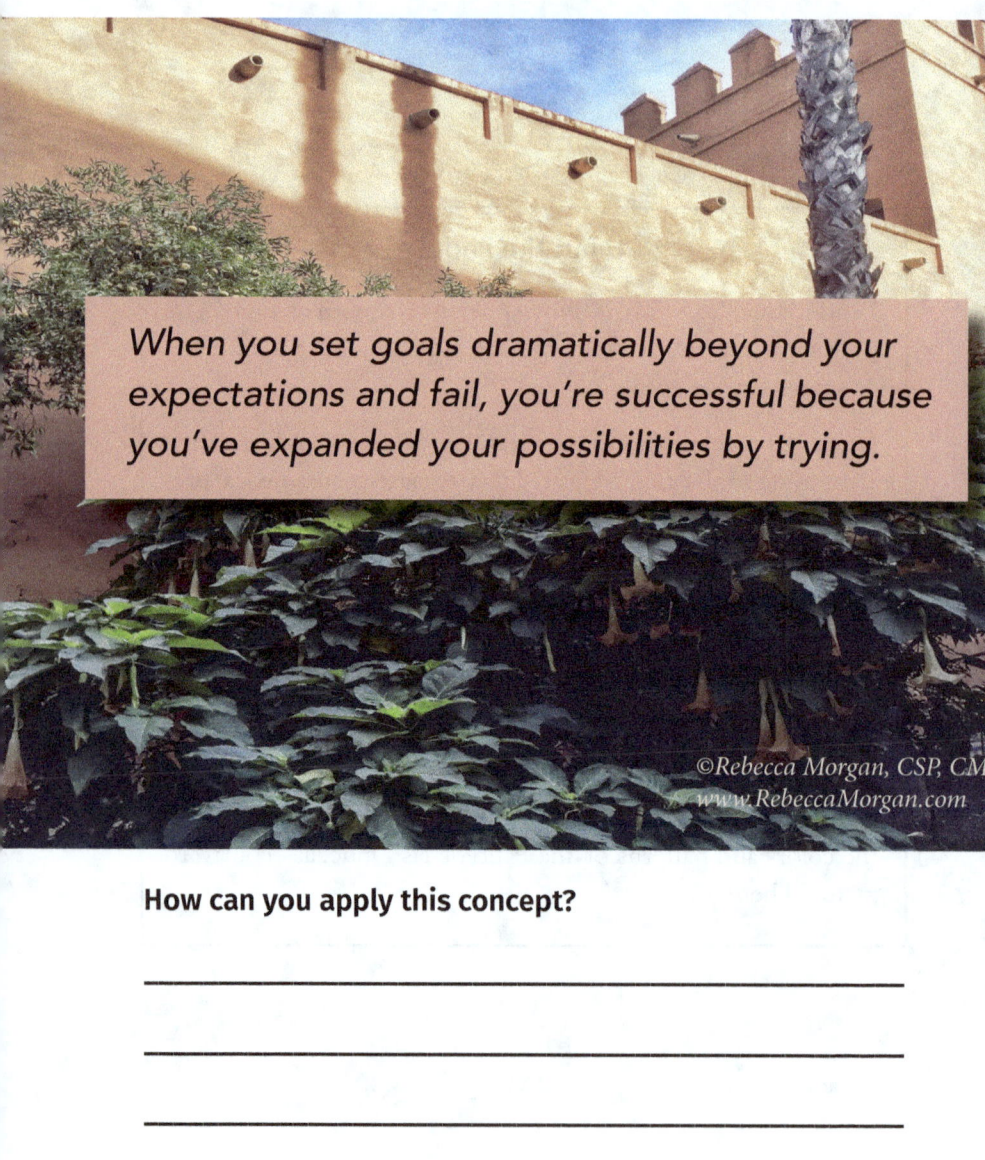

When you set goals dramatically beyond your expectations and fail, you're successful because you've expanded your possibilities by trying.

©Rebecca Morgan, CSP, CMC
www.RebeccaMorgan.com

How can you apply this concept?

_____

_____

_____

_____

Don't Focus on Reaching Your Goals

Traditional advice is to set stretch goals, a tad beyond what you believe you can achieve, then celebrate when you've achieved them.

I have a different perspective. Don't focus on if you achieve them. Set audacious goals and look at who you have to become in order to achieve what you previously thought was not possible. Then celebrate your new habits, attitude or wisdom garnered from stretching way beyond what you thought was possible, even if you didn't make the goal.

A gal pal shared that her shy, seven-year-old daughter was setting out to sell Girl Scout cookies. She asked her daughter how many she thought she could sell. "Eight boxes" was the response. My friend felt her daughter was shooting a bit low, and said, "How about trying to sell 16 boxes?" The little girl nodded that she'd try.

Off she went to knock on neighbors' doors. Soon she burst back into the house, "Mommy, I've sold 22 boxes!" She had to overcome her shyness and she accomplished way beyond she originally thought. She sold 160 boxes!

Many years ago, late on Sunday night at the end of a three-day intense personal-growth weekend, we were asked to share how many guests we'd be bringing to the graduation night two days hence. A few of the 150 in attendance raised their hands and we heard, "One," "Three" "Five" or a rare "Ten" — at which point there was much cheering and applause for someone so willing to commit to a large number aloud. I thought, "If I got my best friend, her husband and my mother, I could get 3, so maybe I should say 5." Then something came over me. I saw that it wasn't about actually achieving bringing the number of guests you'd publicly declared, but more about the growth it would involve to go way beyond what I thought was possible.

I stood and declared, "One hundred." I don't remember, but I imagine there were gasps.

The next morning I arose early to see how close I could get to 100. I found I had to alter the invitation from just "please come" or "I'd appreciate your being there" to "It would mean a lot to me if you were there" then expounding on why this person was important to me and what the weekend learning's had meant to me. I dialed and dialed and had conversations with people I hadn't spoken to in a while. I sincerely told them what had transpired for me that weekend and invited them to share the celebration.

By the end of the second day, the last person confirmed minutes before I left for the celebration. I had 22 people show up.

My lesson was that most of us aim low — I certainly know I did. There's a lot of cultural pressure to achieve what one has publicly promised. And we celebrate achieving even modest goals as if they were huge stretches. There's typically no acknowledgement for not achieving goals, even when what was accomplished went way beyond the initial safe goal. Safe goals save face; stretch goals help you achieve a bit more, but audacious goals create shifts in who you are.

In my calls, I had to dig deep and share from a place I hadn't before with many of my contacts. I saw how our relationship then deepened not only in that conversation, but forever. I liked the shift as we were being less superficial and more intimate in sharing things that truly mattered.

So see if you can shift to celebrating who you've become when you make an outrageous, unreasonable, "unachievable" goal. You may find you not only like the person who emerges as you make every attempt to accomplish what you set out, but that your relationships improve — plus you'll most like achieve more.

About the Photo

Meandering through Seville's The Real Alcázar in the late afternoon, I was delighted to come upon the garden at the end of my self-guided tour. Photographers call this time the golden hour as the sun casts soft rays.

The orange brugmansia flowers matched the walls perfectly. I wondered if they were planted to match the walls or the walls were painted to match them.

Small surprises like this prompt me to raise my camera. I like capturing life's small surprises. Often we don't think to snap a photo during life's big moments. Our memorializing images that catch our eye spawn memories of larger events.

For example, I have no photos of our group's trip to the Arab Baths, a 15-minute walk from our rental home. Yet sitting in the rooftop hot tub overlooking the city was a delightful experience.

I have no photos of us biking around town on a beautiful sunny autumn day. Nor a delicious dinner of tapas. Nor numerous other experiences in Seville.

But I'm grateful for the photos which remind me of other parts of the visit.

Leaderful Listening™

Great leaders strive to fully understand others' ideas and perspectives. They respectfully ask probing questions without arguing.

©Rebecca Morgan, CSP, CMC
www.RebeccaMorgan.com

How can you apply this concept?

_____
_____
_____
_____
_____

Leaderful Listening

In leadership training, participants are typically told how important listening is. Yet few heed the advice.

I can understand why. Often, it's because we already think we are good listeners. But how a leader listens is more crucial than one's listening style as a peer.

Leaders' everyday behaviors have gravitas and impact. Subtleties and nuances can be misinterpreted and blown out of proportion. The simple act of pushing back on an idea can send a leader's direct report into a tizzy. Leaders have to be much more mindful of how they respond to ideas offered by their direct reports.

I call this "leaderful listening." I learned how to listen better as a leader from doing it wrong.

When I was in my first year on the board of my national professional association, I thought I was a good leader. But I had a lot to learn.

Tom, a long-time member approached me to suggest that our national convention should always be in his home city, San Francisco. I proceeded to tell him it was too expensive, our members liked to go to different cities each year, and there weren't a lot of hotels that could accommodate the quantity of meeting rooms we need. Case closed.

I was essentially saying it was a stupid idea.

Is that how a good leader would listen. No!

I could have gently probed, "Tom, that's an interesting idea. I appreciate your bringing this idea to me. I always want to be open to new ideas that will serve our members.

"I know San Francisco is the second top destination in the world, so I can see the appeal. I need some help thinking through a few concerns the board will have."

"Even with group discounts, San Francisco hotel rooms are costlier than our members are used to paying. They are price sensitive and don't attend our events if they hotel room price seems too high. How do you think we could mitigate this being an issue so we don't lose attendees?"

> *When you apply leaderful listening, people feel valued*

"Our members say they like visiting different cities around the country, so how could we entice them to come back to the same city over and over?"

"One of our challenges is finding enough hotel meeting space. Our members aren't keen on going to a nearby convention center. Do you know of large hotels that have a good number of meeting rooms?"

In my original approach, how likely would Tom offer other ideas? If this is my standard way of responding to new ideas, his willingness to offer more is close to zero.

By helping Tom understand the concerns and enlisting him to think through the solutions, he becomes an ally. He feels valued rather than shut down.

Even ideas that seem dumb when first offered can morph into great ideas by thinking though the possibilities. The new idea can shift your paradigm by causing you to approach the situation differently. You want to encourage fresh approaches, not squelch them.

How can you become a more leaderful listener?

- ✦ Acknowledge the person for offering new ideas, no matter if you think it's a good one or not.
- ✦ Ask questions rather than shut down new ideas.
- ✦ Engage the other to help come up with solutions.
- ✦ Ensure your tone is gentle when you probe, not argumentative.

About the Photo

In the decades I've been a professional speaker, I've found it difficult to find a photographer who I think captures me. I was hopeful when I saw a colleague's head shots that made her shine. The only issue was that Warren Jordan, the photographer, is in Colorado and I'm in California.

Luckily, I was planning to visit Colorado and arranged an outside shoot that he said would allow for some more interesting shots than a studio.

Warren selected a park in Parker, a suburb of Denver, for our session. We moved around several areas to get different looks. I brought several tops and a jacket to mix it up.

I loved the results. I started to incorporate his photos into my quote memes and slides.

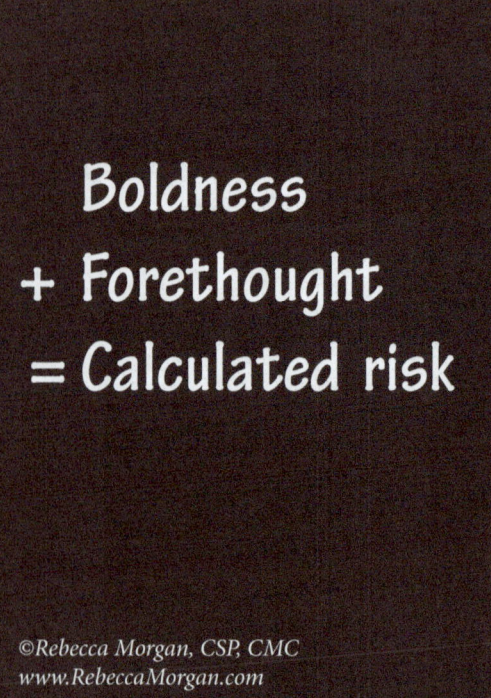

Boldness
+ Forethought
= Calculated risk

©Rebecca Morgan, CSP, CMC
www.RebeccaMorgan.com

How can you apply this concept?

_____
_____
_____
_____
_____

Take Calculated Risks

> *"Take calculated risks. That is quite different from being rash."* — George S. Patton from a letter to Cadet George S. Patton IV, June 6, 1944

Taking calculated risks means boldness with forethought. It means weighing the outcome and avoiding unwise action. A calculated risk might be giving a presentation to your boss' peers, telling someone they have a habit that annoys you, volunteering for a project you've never done before, or trying a new sport.

We can learn to take calculated risks, and they get easier with repeated attempts. Eventually you learn that you can pick yourself up and continue even if your boldness causes you to fall flat.

Morgan W. McCall Jr., coauthor of *What It Takes: Decision Makers at Work*, conducted a study comparing 20 successful Fortune 500 executives with 20 whose careers hadn't been successful. One difference he found was that the achievers were secure enough to admit their fallibility, and they handled their mistakes with poise and grace. They analyzed their mistakes and learned from them, but they didn't become obsessed. "Executive achievers don't dwell on their mistakes and aren't afraid to take risks for fear of failing again," says McCall.

Many times it has been difficult for me to overcome my initial paralysis when faced with a risky challenge. Years ago when I entered the pension business, my boss assigned me to call on one tax attorney per day. Attorneys intimidated me. I almost had a heart attack.

My comfort zone was narrow. I felt comfortable calling on other insurance agents to ask them to recommend our services, but that was not where the real business was. The business came from tax attorneys and accountants.

After a few months of stressful and anxiety-ridden calls, my comfort zone expanded, and I was comfortable calling attorneys. But it wasn't easy to overcome my self-doubts and intimidation. I learned from reading, workshops, and experienced friends that all growth occurs outside the comfort zone.

Now as I enter new areas requiring a stretch of my comfort zone, I've learned to ask myself these questions. Use them to help you act outside your comfort zone. When deciding to take a risk, write your responses to these six questions.

1. What is the worst that can happen?

When I was asked to call on attorneys I was afraid I would:

- make a fool of myself
- be asked questions I didn't know how to answer
- be kicked out of their offices
- be embarrassed
- be told that I was wasting their time.

These are disaster fantasies. We think of the worst possible outcomes, whether they are realistic or not.

2. What is the likelihood of this happening?

Be realistic. The fear may distort your objectivity, but try. Often you will find the likelihood to be small.

3. If this did happen, could I live with the outcome?

If yes, go for it. If no, then strategize another plan. I decided yes, I could live with someone throwing me out of their office. I wouldn't enjoy it, it would be uncomfortable and emotionally painful, but I could live with it. I'd learn from my mistake and not make it again.

I once had an appointment with an attorney to solicit him as a center of influence. He was so hostile during the meeting that he stood behind his desk the whole time and never asked me to sit down. So I conducted the entire interview standing!

Did this experience leave me alive? Yes. Was it uncomfortable? Extremely. Did I learn from it? Yes — I was better prepared to deal with hostility and rejection.

4. What am I afraid won't happen?

Sometimes we fear what won't happen as much as what will happen. If I called on successful attorneys, I was afraid that I wouldn't get any referrals from these centers of influence, or that I wouldn't establish a positive image for myself and my firm. Repeat questions 2 and 3 to get past this particular point of resistance.

5. What are the benefits to my not taking this risk?

- ✦ It's comfortable at my current comfort zone. No pain.
- ✦ I don't have to think much. I can do my job on automatic pilot.
- ✦ I'm making enough money to get by.
- ✦ If I try something new, I might fail.
- ✦ I'm at the top of the heap right now.
- ✦ If I try something now I could fall on my face.
- ✦ I'm too old to change.

After you defend all your excuses, focus on the benefits to taking the risk.

6. What are the benefits to my taking this risk?

- ✦ I would learn new skills.

- ✦ I will feel better about myself because I'm trying something outside of my comfort zone.
- ✦ I could be wildly successful!

The late Doug Hooper, author of *You Are What You Think*, said "Anything that comes up in your life that will be to your betterment, say 'yes' to it immediately."

Don't think about how uncomfortable you will be, or that you've never tried this before, or that you don't think you can do it. Instead, work through the six questions, weigh the outcome, and more often than you think, you'll benefit from risking a yes.

> *All growth occurs outside your comfort zone*

About the Photo

On a visit to Adelaide, Australia, my friend Derrick treated me to a trip to Cleland Wildlife Park where I met this bird called a cassowary. Luckily, it was behind a fence as they are said to be one of the most dangerous birds in the world.

Its beauty captivated me. Such rich blue as well as bright colors on its neck. And those golden eyes! It's a large bird, coming up to my shoulders.

The top of its head is hard (I'm told), similar to humans' fingernails.

While traveling in the rainforest of northeast Australia, I encountered road signs with cassowary images warning motorists to look out for the birds. I was told they will attack humans, thus the need for the signs.

I'm glad I met this cassowary — and that it was behind a fence.

Diligently track your agreements. Keep your promises. Finish on time.

You'll stand out a true professional.

©Rebecca Morgan, CSP, CMC
www.RebeccaMorgan.com

How can you apply this concept?

_____

_____

_____

_____

_____

Stand Out As a True Professional

What makes someone stand out as a true professional?

Is it their deep knowledge of their job?

Their pleasant attitude and cooperation?

Their willingness to tackle tough topics and projects?

The ability to creatively problem-solve?

Yes. All of these.

Additionally, an area that gets little discussion in management and leadership literature is the high value of diligence at completing what you promise.

Perhaps this is thought to be a given.

Yet how often does a colleague or vendor promise they'll get back to you and they don't? Usually there's nary a heads up that they will be late. They just ghost you and you're left without the critical decision or information you need.

You don't realize they've gone poof until you are under the gun to complete the project with the missing info. You are now stressed because they let you down.

This happens so much it's barely acknowledged by the culprit. "Oops. It slipped my mind," he says, without a word of apology or acknowledgment of how his lack of follow through has left you in a lurch.

"I thought I sent that to you," is another oft-heard comment. I always wonder if she knows full well she didn't and just doesn't want to fess up.

How can you avoid being one of these flakes? It's really not that hard. Yet I'm amazed how few people consistently abandon their commitments.

Diligently track your agreements.

> When you agree to take on a task, write it down wherever you track your to-do's. Make it easy on yourself by telling your device's smart assistant (Siri or Google) to add the item to your calendar or to-do list. Note the due date and time so you don't let it slip.

Keep your promises.

> Honoring your promises shows you are trustworthy. That you value the relationship. You hold yourself to a standard of acting with integrity.

Finish on time.

> Strive to complete the task not only on time, but ahead of when you promised, if possible. You wow people when you do this.

> If you see you'll not be able to complete the task within the time frame you promised, let the person know. Then she can make other arrangements to fill the gap you've now left gaping.

There's a reason the phrase "Your word is your bond" has survived for centuries. When you consistently keep your word, you demonstrate your integrity. When you practice this kind of rigor and diligence to your agreements, people trust you. They want to work with you. You get raises, promotions and sales. Life is better.

About the Photo

My traveling buddy, Susan, and I were in week two of a three-week trip to five European countries. She'd arranged for us to stay with her cousin, Louise, for a few nights in Luxembourg. Departing from the Netherlands via train, we passed through Belgium.

That evening, Louise and her family took us to a restaurant in the southeast corner of the country. After dinner, they asked if we wanted to visit two more countries that evening. We had no idea we were only a few miles from where Germany and France border Luxembourg. In 15 minutes, we zipped through the tip of both so we could say we'd been to five countries in one day!

Although Louise is a busy attorney and had a toddler in tow, she took us around the country the next day. It's such a little country, it didn't take long! One of the highlights was taking a chair lift to the top of a hill to view

Vianden Castle. It was closed that day but so we viewed the outside, and I snapped this photo at the bottom of the chair lift. I loved the trees in bloom in the foreground.

I am always grateful when my friends' friends and relatives treat me as one of their friends, too, and take steps to make my visit memorable. Thus it was with Louise. I now do more to pay it forward with my friends' friends.

How can you apply this concept?

_____
_____
_____
_____
_____

Is Your Superpower Recognizing Others' Superpowers?

Identifying one's "superpower" has become a hot topic. We are encouraged to identify where we excel. This is not always an easy task. Most of us are either oblivious to how we stand out, or at the other end of the continuum, think have more competence than we actually do.

Thus it's a challenge to figure out our brilliance. It helps to ask a cross section of friends, peers and your boss or clients to see if a trend appears.

I recently asked an in-tact group to share the superpowers they saw in individual teammates. This was a moving exercise, resulting in the CEO in tears. She said she had no idea people thought she possessed so many admirable qualities.

> *Her appreciation gave me a new perspective*

Sometimes our superpower is recognizing the brilliance of others. However, we don't often tell them, as we figure they already know. Don't make this mistake! People often don't see their excellence because they take it for granted. It takes no thought for them, they do it naturally.

Or someone may think you have an asset when you think it's a liability. It takes someone else to point out the thing that you don't value is highly valuable to others.

For example, I was traveling in Asia for several weeks and needed to do laundry for my last few days. What prompts most people to want to do laundry? Undies! I couldn't find a convenient laundromat, but remembered a nearby street merchant selling women's undergarments. I approached the petite women who I assumed spoke little English. I pointed to the lingerie on her table, then to my prodigious hips, and held my hands wide, like showing the size of a fish. "Giant?" I asked. She smiled, pointed to my hips and said, "Nice!"

I was taken aback. I'd never considered my wide hips to be "nice." But I immediately realized that for someone who didn't have curves and would have liked some, they would be nice. I hadn't appreciated something that she admired. It gave me a new perspective.

Help others appreciate something you admire about them but they may not. Make a habit of sharing what you admire, appreciate, or acknowledge in others. You will be more connected. And the receiver may shift their perspective on what they may have long held as a liability.

About the Photo

My traveling buddy, Jana, and I decided to spend a few days in Hong Kong on our way home from other countries in Southeast Asia. It was her first visit to Hong Kong but I'd been there once a few years before. There were sights I wanted to explore and a few I wanted to revisit.

We stayed on the Hong Kong side, so we took the Star Ferry across the harbor. Steps from the exit is a shopping mall that was festooned with Chinese New Year lanterns. The density of the pink-red lanterns delighted me, so I started taking photos. I liked this one the best.

That evening, we wedged ourselves into the crowd snuggled up to the edge of the water to watch the nightly laser show through drizzling rain. Music played through loudspeakers, timed to the lasers dancing on buildings on both sides of the harbor.

The red-sailed Chinese junk boats, also known as Aqua Luna, sat in the middle of the harbor, allowing their passengers to enjoy the show from a unique perspective.

On my last trip, this time with Susan, it was a cold January night, so our friend Ron suggested we meet him at the Hotel Intercontinental. When we arrived (after a 90-minute foot massage), he'd reserved a table for us next to the windows overlooking the water. Thanks to Ron's foresight and the best hot chocolate of my life, this viewing of the laser show was the best ever.

I never tire of this show and have made it a point to witness it every time I visit this beautiful city.

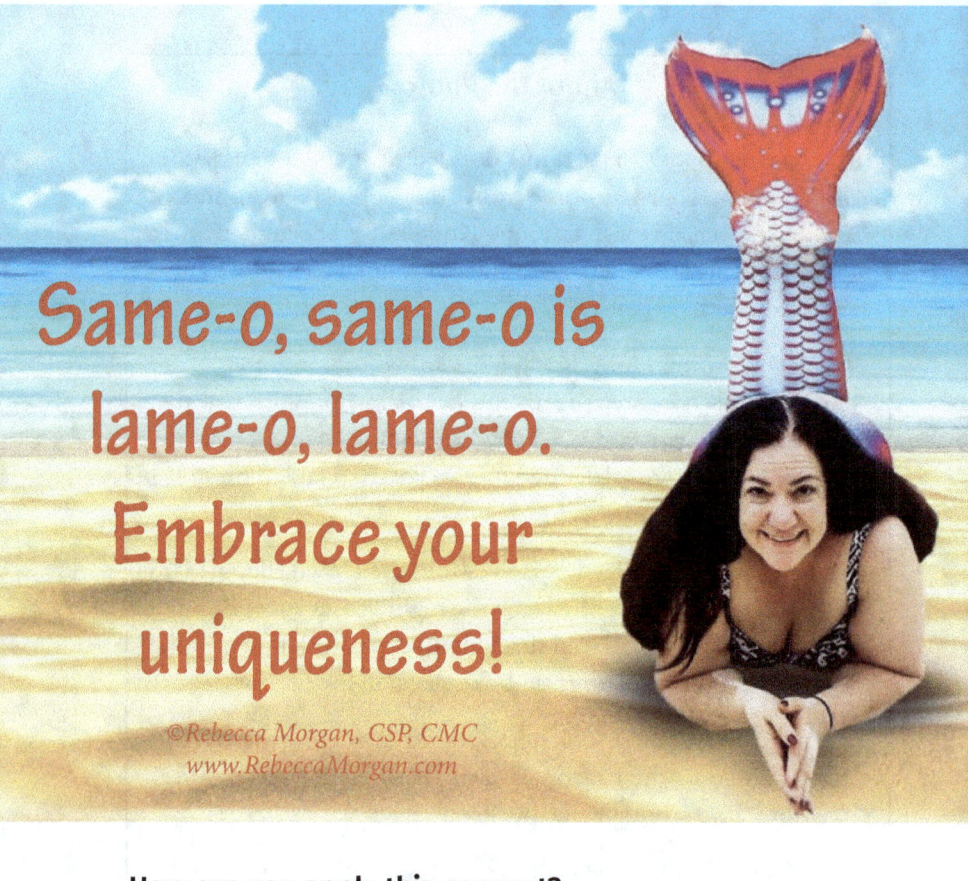

How can you apply this concept?

_____

_____

_____

_____

_____

Same-o, Same-o is Lame-o, Lame-o. Embrace Your Uniqueness!

Odd. Different. Weird.

Have you been called one (or more) of these? If so, you're far from alone.

This may be a key to your success.

Perhaps you've embraced your uniqueness. You own it. You love who you are and don't let naysayers force you into blandness.

Your unusualness sets you apart so you can shine. You are memorable.

But only if you have the courage to be true to who you are. To let your distinctive quirkiness show. To not hide, even if you are from a family or culture that reinforces that the tall poppy gets sheared.

The difficulty in celebrating your uncommonness can be believing your unusual traits are valued. You bring a new perspective to the meeting, game, class, family, or company. It may be hard to find a place where you are valued. Especially if others laud uniformity and homogeneity.

Another challenge is knowing when one-of-a-kind and remarkable crosses the line to weird, peculiar, strange, or bizarre. This line is subjective, of course, but you don't want to be seen as so odd that you are shunned.

Finding your "peeps" is key to embracing your matchlessness. These people will accept, love and perhaps even promote you to others.

Think of well-known people you admire. Most likely, they each posses some uncommon characteristic. Whether it's their voice, dance moves, style, talent, intelligence, courage, perseverance, drive, altruism, authenticity, oration, athleticism, or whatever, they accept who they are and offer their talents to the world. Their fans would be sad if the person chose to not share their gifts anymore.

Lady Gaga is an example of boldly owning her disparate elements to become a huge star. She combined a powerful singing voice, thoughtful lyrics, bold stage presence, and flamboyant fashion style to become a worldwide sensation, even before she turned 30. She encourages fans to courageously be themselves, especially with songs like, "Born This Way." Millions of people who were told they are — or consider themselves to be — misfits have been touched by her music.

My family did not value unusualness. They didn't like to get attention or stand out. My enthusiasm for student leadership, acting, and choir soloist was met with demeaning comments and demands to end these extracurricular activities. Luckily, I was encouraged by my teachers to pursue these passions and I'm glad I did. The confidence and skills I garnered have served me throughout my career.

Here are two exercises to help you identify and champion your uniqueness.

- ✦ If you are unsure of your uncommon gifts, make a list of what you think may be your unconventional traits. Ask for input from people who support you. Do they think these traits are rare and should be encouraged? Or do they cross the line into annoying?
- ✦ Add to the list anything you think is odd, peculiar, or eccentric about you — anything you have yet to celebrate. Ask your pals to help you see the value in these traits. Look for where the combination of these can help you shine even more.

About the Photo

Boracay Island in the Philippines, has been voted one of the most beautiful sights in the world. Miles of white-sand beaches and warm, teal water beckon you.

Our group was visiting to conduct seminars for the Discovery Shores Boracay resort, as well as for some relaxation. After my morning seminar, we had the afternoon off. The women wanted me to join them at the Mermaid Academy.

When I asked what was entailed, the gals said we'd don mermaid flippers and learn some mermaid tricks in the water. This sounded good to me.

When we arrived, we were asked to pick out our mermaid tails — hand painted stretchy fabric with built-in flippers fused into one unit. These went over our bathing suite bottoms. The instructor directed us to pose lying in the sand for our photos.

Wait, what?! We are having pictures taken in our bathing suits? No! I wouldn't have come had I known this.

Wanting to be a good sport, however, I got past my discomfort and posed with my gal pals. I knew we could delete any photos we didn't like. The instructor knew how to put us in poses so we looked our best. I loved our photos.

Then we inched ourselves on our rears, like worms, to the water's edge. We could not stand up because of the flippers. The cool waves were bracing! The water slapped us in the face as we tried to get deep enough to swim. We were screeching with laughter. Beachgoers gathered around, recording video of these aging mermaids trying to get into the water. I turned my face away as I didn't want to be on anyone's Facebook feed!

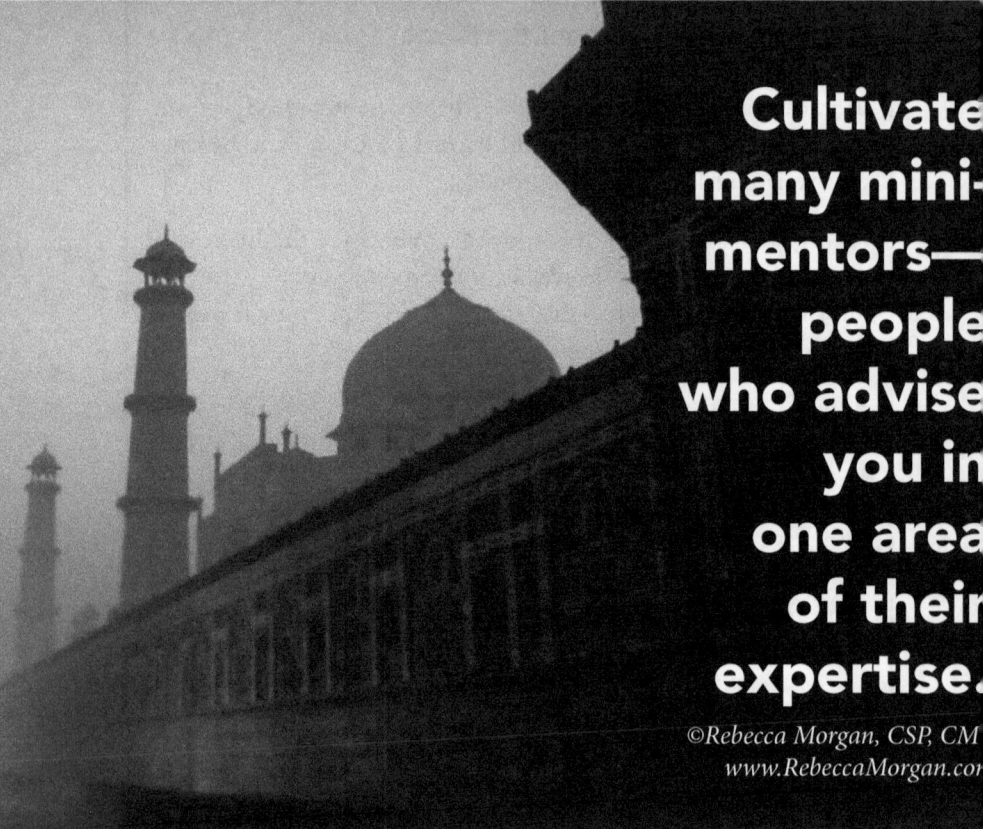

Cultivate many mini-mentors—people who advise you in one area of their expertise.

©Rebecca Morgan, CSP, CM
www.RebeccaMorgan.com

How can you apply this concept?

_____
_____
_____
_____
_____

Cultivate Many Mini-Mentors

What is a mini-mentor? Someone who advises you in one area of their expertise.

Cultivate many of them. Why?

If you don't know someone well, most people will be reticent to say yes to your request to be your mentor. They are concerned about the time and emotional energy it might take.

However, if you ask if they would provide guidance in one finite area of their expertise, most will say yes.

For example, early in my career I had so much to learn. How can I secure speaking or training engagements? How do I get articles published? How do I get my book published? How do I improve my slides? How can I tell better stories in my presentation? The list was long.

One mentor would have been overwhelmed educating me on so many areas. Although a few people offered to mentor me, I consulted them judiciously as I didn't want to inundate them with my many questions.

Instead, I asked those more senior to me if I may ask them a few questions on a specific area where I knew they were accomplished. Every one said yes.

Before I reached out to see if s/he would be willing to answer a few questions on the topic, I researched their experience in that topic. I then prepared my questions in advance, set up a phone call or coffee, and began with what I knew of their expertise in that area.

I could tell they were pleased I had taken the time to examine their work in that area, and wasn't just asking broad questions. I also didn't start by talking about me. I'd explain how I'd used their work as a model, but was stuck and would welcome their advice.

I never asked for anything other than advice — not introductions to their contacts, a quote for a book, a critique of my demo video. I didn't want anyone feeling I was taking advantage of my connection with them.

After our conversation, I'd send a handwritten thank-you card acknowledging their generous advice and time. I would also follow up with updates on my results of using their advice so they knew their words were taken seriously.

> *Mini-mentors mean many people will cheer you on*

Some mini-mentors became full-on mentors, taking a broader interest in my career and accomplishments. Some initiated congratulations on my achievements, or to see how they might provide more help.

None asked for a cent, even when I offered to pay for their sending me their latest book or other resource materia.

Few people are eager to take on the responsibility of mentoring someone they don't know well. But if you develop relationships with mini-mentors, your growth will take less time, and you'll have many people cheering you on.

About the Photo

The Taj Mahal, in Agra, India, is magnificent, even at sunrise. And even when viewed from the back.

I awoke before sunrise the day after my group arrived in Agra. I couldn't get back to sleep, so I went to the hotel restaurant to see if it was open for breakfast. It wasn't. But a few others of our group were gathered there, also afflicted with jet lag.

One of us hatched a plan to go to the Taj Mahal right away, to be one of the first into the shrine. We had no idea when it opened, but knew it would be more interesting than the hotel lobby.

We hailed a tuk tuk, the local transportation. Within minutes we arrived at the entrance. It was closed.

A gray-haired gentleman beckoned us in broken English to follow him down a rock-strewn walkway bordering the wall encompassing the grounds. We were cautious since it was still dark and we had no idea where he was taking us. We quickly decided no harm would come to us as we could hear worshippers at morning prayers in the adjacent mosque. Two of us followed him.

After a short walk we were rewarded with this image of the Taj Mahal from the river as the dawn was breaking. I'd not seen a photograph from this perspective so I started snapping.

I have other, more traditional photos of the Taj Mahal from the front, but there are people everywhere. Even arriving at opening does not guarantee you will be rewarded with a pristine shot without tourists. You're more likely to get that photo from the back.

Harness the Power of Commitment

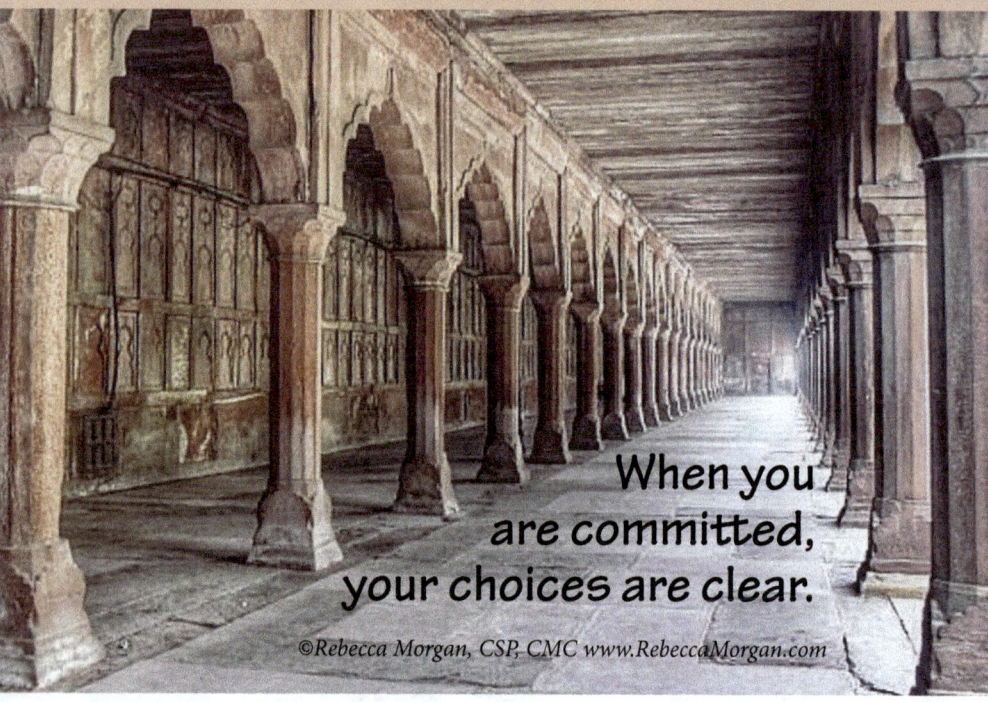

When you are committed, your choices are clear.

©Rebecca Morgan, CSP, CMC www.RebeccaMorgan.com

How can you apply this concept?

_____
_____
_____
_____
_____

Harness the Power of Commitment

"Do or die!"
"Don't give up the ship!"
"Damn the torpedoes and full speed ahead!"

Military expressions are valuable during war when the price of failure is death. But they lose impact in our business or private life: failure is not quite as final. However, these sayings are based on a principle that applies to all aspects of our lives: commitment.

This commitment to one's goals is, for me, the most important rule for success. Without it, we fall prey to procrastination, bad habits, laziness, rationalization and a host of goal-defeating problems.

Commitment is a strong word — much stronger than "agreement." If I agree to meet you for a movie, I have three options — keeping my agreement, cancelling, or changing it. If I commit to meeting you, I will meet you no matter what.

Commitments often require sacrifice in order to achieve a goal. If your goal is to be self-employed, you will probably need to sacrifice an active social life for awhile.

When I started my business, I worked 14-hour days, six to seven days a week. I was totally committed to my goal. I dreamed of owning my own successful seminar company. I wanted to help others become the best they could be. I wanted to share my knowledge of the universal laws of success and make a living doing it.

I worked for someone else from 9:00-5:00, then I either designed, researched or presented a seminar in the evening. During lunch hours, I made phone calls to prospective clients. On weekends, I wrote my client proposals and contracts.

Life Is a Self-Designed, Personal Growth Seminar

I was busy, but happy. Sure, it was exhausting, but I was able to achieve my goal of being self-supporting in my own business in just one year, instead of the 2-3 I projected. I owe my success to my commitment to my goal.

I haven't achieved all my goals. At one time I wanted to be an interpreter at the United Nations. I took courses in Spanish, French, and Japanese, but then I gave up. For many years, I talked about learning to fly an airplane. I talked, but never took the first step. Looking back on my life, I can see the difference between goals I was committed to and ones I wasn't: I've succeeded at my committed goals.

When you are committed to your goals, attaining them is easier. Your choices are clearer. If your goal is to become the top salesperson in the company, then the choice between going home when everyone else does or staying an extra hour and to make ten cold calls may not be easy, but you know what you have to do, and you do it. If your goal is to lose 15 pounds, your choice between having a carrot or a piece of carrot cake becomes clearer. When you are not committed to your goals, your choices become hazy.

Being committed means doing whatever it takes. Commitment does not mean walking all over fellow workers or stabbing people in the back to attain your goals. It does mean making those extra phone calls or jogging around the block or working long hours even when you don't feel like it.

When the first Neiman-Marcus store burned to the ground in 1913, 5.5 years after it had opened, the owners could have easily collected the insurance money and gone off to do other things. But Herbert Marcus was the dreamer of the partners, and he persuaded them to collect the insurance money, canvas the family for additional funds and build a larger store.

They could have given up, but they didn't. Marcus kept the dream alive and did what it took to create an internationally known specialty store.

Life Is a Self-Designed, Personal Growth Seminar

Marcus was committed.

Lee Iacocca did what it took to save the ailing Chrysler Corporation. He even took only $1 a year in salary in order to leave the capital in the company. It worked. Now Chrysler is a successful auto maker again. Iacocca was committed.

Being committed to our goals often isn't easy, and it takes considerable time and effort. That's why we make so few commitments and often have such trouble keeping them. Americans in general are impatient; we don't like to stand in line or wait; we want what we want right now. If everyone in America were promised a million dollars, tax free, for meditating one hour every day, from 5-6 a.m. for two years, I believe a high percentage would never collect the money. "Too much trouble," we'd say. That's the trouble with commitment — it's too much trouble.

Commitment requires strong self-discipline, and a persistent inner voice to urge us on. Self-discipline grows out of our commitment to our goals. Your inner voice may also conflict with your stated goals. This voice tries to fight commitments and wants to get out of them. It may say, "Oh, go home early. You've worked hard. You deserve it." Like a soldier facing the enemy, we face our own inner enemies — "I'll do it tomorrow." "I can't do it." When we accept a commitment, it should be with "do or die" determination, otherwise it's only a weak agreement. Real commitment takes courage, sacrifice, and perseverance.

If you are able to hang in there and work toward your dreams and your goals a little bit each day, you will have them. Commit yourself to the attainment of your goals, and develop the self-discipline to do what it takes. As an added benefit, you'll achieve the satisfaction and confidence that comes with your success.

When you are committed, anything is possible.

How can you apply this concept?

_____

_____

_____

_____

_____

Honesty, Without Caring, Is Abuse

Nearly everyone I've known has said they want honest feedback on areas they can improve.

Hearing this, some perceive it as an invitation to be mean. Sometimes really mean. Insulting. Demeaning. Humiliating.

Abusive.

No matter how much we say we want honest, blunt feedback, nearly everyone appreciates receiving constructive criticism couched in a way that doesn't leave the receiver feeling bullied or wounded. Verbal abuse often has long-lasting affects — sometimes for decades.

As the feedback giver, think about how you want the person to feel afterwards. Even if *you* can stomach blunt feedback, not everyone can. Even if they say they can, feelings of inadequacy can linger long after the interaction. Harsh words echo in the receiver's ears.

When you care about the receiver, you carefully choose your words and tone. You select neutral words, not inflammatory ones. Instead of "You really screwed up," you say, "I know this task is difficult. Few people do it well at first. Let's go over the procedure again so you do even better next time."

Is this coddling? Too namby-pamby? For a few people, yes. For many, it allows them to keep their dignity intact while learning how to do better.

Before you open your mouth or put fingers to the keyboard to offer honest feedback, pause and ask yourself how you can show caring in your communication. The receiver may not express their appreciation for your efforts, but you'll know you've raised your level of communication and kept the relationship undamaged.

About the Photo
Harness the Power of Commitment

Our group of 17 women were enjoying exploring the places Jana, my friend and the group's leader, had picked for us.

She'd arranged for us to visit the hill top City Palace in Jaipur, India. To navigate the steep hill, we sat on raised platforms atop elephants, two per animal.

The elephants ambled up a walkway, one right behind the other. Their heads were painted with bright colors, and our seat was perched on a colorful rug.

At the top, we took in the beauty of the palace, which was beautifully preserved. This hallway was striking. Imagine the spaces between pillars decorated with colorful silk curtains and couches.

We saw a wall with holes for the palace inhabitants to watch the events taking place in the courtyard below. They weren't allowed to interact with the peasants, so they could be a part of the scene without talking to any of them.

One of the details I remember from the tour is that the king had so many concubines, he had to set a day a week to mediating disputes between them. He needed a concubine manager!

About the Photo
Honesty, Without Caring, Is Abuse

Our group had been visiting our projects that serve underprivileged women and children in Laos and northern Thailand. Before we left the area, we had to visit the Red Lotus Lake (Nong Han Kumphawapi Lake) in Udon Thani, Thailand.

The lake's name is a bit of a misnomer. The flowers are really tropical water lilies, not lotus, and the color is really pink, not red. No matter, it is a spectacular sight, even if it's only available during the cool months.

Our group clambered aboard a small boat for a 90-minute tour around the lake. Within a few minutes, we were surrounded by beautiful pink lilies as far as the eye can see. The freshwater lake is approximately 5 miles long and 2 miles wide, so that's a lot of lilies.

The boats follow a marked trail to disturb as few flowers as possible. We stop periodically so we can stand to take selfies with the lake in the background.

I'm continually surprised that some of my favorite experiences are those I had never heard of until I'm standing in front of it. The Red Lotus Lake is one of the many I am grateful to have experienced.

How can you apply this concept?

_____

_____

_____

_____

_____

Give Verbal Hugs

We are mindful about touching people, yet we want to show we care by embracing others,

Try a verbal hug instead.

This sincere acknowledgment is said to make the receiver feel warm, loved, and honored. For example, instead of greeting someone with the trite "How are you?" try "It's so good to see you," or, if it's true, "You're looking great."

When ending a telephone conversation, instead of "See you later," try "It was really good to talk to you," or "It was great to catch up with you," or "I'm glad things are going well for you."

Make a point to tell the person one behavior or characteristic you admire about them, "I always admire your patience with challenging people." Reinforce a success with, "You worked hard. You deserve it."

Use a verbal hug to share someone something you admire, appreciate or acknowledge about them, without it being about their looks. "I like your eyes" has little impact as he had nothing to do with the shape or color of his eyes. "I admire your careful wording when you're giving me feedback." means much more.

A verbal massage is even more powerful. Have a group of friends, family or associates take one minute sharing sincere, positive characteristics about one of your group. Then focus on the next person for one minute. Comments like "nice shirt," or "you're not as obnoxious as you used to be," aren't what we're looking for here.

When you're the recipient, you'll feel great.

Who can you "hug" today?

Vulnerability + Strength = Personal Power™

©Rebecca Morgan, CSP, CMC
www.RebeccaMorgan.com

How can you apply this concept?

_____
_____
_____
_____
_____

Vulnerability + Strength = Personal Power

Some people are drawn to forceful leaders. Others appreciate leaders who have a gentler approach.

I — and many others — find the combination of vulnerability plus strength is compelling. Many people feel connected to others who are willing to show humility, admit when they are wrong, demonstrate heartfelt emotions, and express sincere caring for others.

However, the leader can't be timid or cowardly. Saying, "That's just the way I am" does not show awareness that your behaviors harm others close to you. It's a cop out. Saying, "I've had that bad habit a long time. It will be hard for me to change, but I am willing to focus on changing it as I see it is hurtful."

Vulnerability has to be coupled with strength to obtain respect. Combining the two creates personal power, resulting in leaders many want to follow. How do you balance the two?

- Show vulnerability by apologizing when you have made a mistake. Vow to do better in the future.

- Apologize when you've done something that negatively affected someone. Couple it with courage by adding, "And I won't ever do that again."

- When you know someone is struggling, gently ask how you can support them, then do whatever you can to help. Sometimes they may just want a compassionate listener or a hug. Or you can merely lighten their load, or do something you know will help.

They key is to be willing to show your humanity. Many people will appreciate this and want to follow you.

About the Photo
Give Verbal Hugs

I was plotting an eight-week, seven-country speaking tour, including some countries I'd not visited. One of them was New Zealand. Reaching out to my Kiwi pal, I asked them what to do with a few days between engagements,. Several highly recommended I visit Queenstown on the South Island.

During my April visit, this resort town was chilly, with occasional snow and sleet. But that didn't slow me down. I packed as much in as I could in my 2.5 days.

Walking home after a $1/2$-day steamboat ride and lunch across Lake Wakatipu, then a speedboat ride down a mountain river, the sunset stopped me in my tracks. The pink reflecting off the clouds and snow atop The Remarkables mountain range, was, well, remarkable. It's understandable why this range is called the Southern Alps.

I decided to linger to enjoy every moment so stopped at an upstairs cafe overlooking the lake. A 5-year-old boy came to see the view and said hello. Sipping hot chocolate, I struck up a conversation.

I asked his mother if I may give him a sticker — I always carry some with me for kids. I think of myself as a sticker fairy. He squealed with joy, and his sister asked for one, too.

People ask me if it is lonely traveling alone. I find I rarely have a day alone, and this trip was no different. I reach out to professional pals ahead of time to spend time together. They usually like to show me their favorite sites.

On this visit, I stayed with a friend of a pal, who put me up at her charming Airbnb apartment without charging me. Friendly, generous people are everywhere.

About the Photo
Vulnerability + Strength = Personal Power

I've noticed that when I travel, my senses are heightened. I'm more observant, seeing details I would have missed in my home area. I strive to bring my awareness home with me.

When this Monarch butterfly landed on my patio bougainvillea, I not only noticed the exquisiteness in the contrasting colors, I sprung into action.

Grabbing my phone, I began snapping, looking for the perfect shot. Drat, the butterfly's wings are closed. Oops, I snapped too late and it's gone. Channeling Dewitt Jones, I waited for it to return. I was rewarded when it did a few minutes later. Snap. Snap. I finally got this shot with the butterfly's wings outstretched.

I'm reminded of Dewitt's philosophy to capture a photo of something of beauty every day. It's easier when you're away from home. This day, hearing Dewitt's words provided a lovely payoff.

Commit to continuous personal improvement.
Regularly create beneficial chaos.
Continually question your best practices.
Radically shake up elements of your life.

©Rebecca Morgan, CSP, CM
www.RebeccaMorgan.com

How can you apply this concept?

_____

_____

_____

_____

_____

Commit to Continuous Personal Improvement

People I admire strive to become better as a partner, parent, child, friend, boss, coworker or human being. They are continually looking for ways to improve, whether for their relationships, or to create more effective habits for themselves.

I've noticed three ways these people improve themselves.

1. Regularly create beneficial chaos.

Beneficial chaos is when you purposefully destroy something to rebuild it for the better. Changing jobs can be chaotic at first, but you do so to grow professionally. Remodeling your home means going through some chaos for a better result. Even small things, like reorganizing your closet means taking everything out (chaos) to throw out items and organize the remaining ones.

When you intentionally create a big change, you know it will require some patience and discomfort before experiencing the benefit. If you aren't willing to go through this, you will always wonder how life would have been better if you had made the shift.

What have you been wanting to do that you haven't because you're concerned about the chaos it would create? Write down the specific disarray the action might cause and who would be affected. In partnership with them (ideally), map out how you could mitigate the upheaval so it's bearable. Estimate the duration of each stage so you know how long you'll have to muddle through.

A few years ago I remodeled my kitchen, one of my bathrooms and a guest room. I work from home so knew I'd have to work around the sawing, hammering and dust. I arranged the remodel for the summer so I could move my kitchen and work space outside in the pleasant weather. I had a full-sized refrigerator, grill, pots, pans, table and chairs. I washed dishes in my master bathroom. It was actually fun to work and cook outside for the summer. Although I crave order, I knew this was only for a few months and made the best of it.

2. Continually question your best practices.

We think about how to do something the first time then rarely question the process. We habitually accomplish tasks the same way each time: drive to work, brush our teeth, cook an egg, fold clothes, pay bills, etc.

What if we step back and regularly examine our practices? Marie Kondo causes people to think about how they store their clothing so many are now rolling or stacking items on end. Your dentist may cause you to rethink how you brush or floss your teeth. Beautiful, sunny days may inspire you to walk or ride your bike to complete errands.

I travel a lot and have modified my habits so now I pack more effectively and efficiently. I continue to experiment with new methods so my life is less stressful on the road. I've discovered I love to pack as it's like a big jigsaw puzzle!

Each day or week, evaluate something you do without thinking and ask yourself if there's a better way. You'll be surprised by how many habits you can improve, or steps you can eliminate.

3. Radically shake up elements of your life.

Be willing to ask yourself, "What if I ...." I asked myself:
- ✦ What if I made my home office into a guest room?
- ✦ What if I converted my paper files to digital and discarded the paper?

- ✦ What if I got rid of items I haven't used in a few years?
- ✦ What if I listed my new guest room on Airbnb?

I took action based on this series of "What if I" questions. The result has allowed me to meet some great people who stayed in my home, and gave me revenue to contribute to the charities I support.

Friends have rented their home out for a year or more as they traveled. Some have gone back to school in their forties, fifties or sixties. Others have started businesses. Some have ended or started relationships.

Perhaps these examples are too extreme for you. "Radical" for you may mean joining an exercise class and attending regularly. Or enrolling in a course you've wanted to take. Or finding a more scenic way to work, even if it takes a little longer.

Only you can decide what "radical" means to you and how much shake up you can embrace.

The key to committing to continuous personal improvement is being aware of what you're doing (or not doing) and challenging yourself to improve it. It can only make your life better.

About the Photo

My cousins were visiting Monterey from Kansas and they wanted a beautiful hiking spot. I hadn't been to Pt. Lobos in years, even though it was only a 90-minute drive from my house.

The hike along the cliffs was unparalleled in its beauty. The aquamarine sea's gentle swells rocked the seaweed like a baby. We spotted otters and seals bobbing on the surface.

Monterey pines clung to the cliff face, apparently defying gravity, their roots laid bare. We marveled that they hadn't tumbled to the sea below. I wondered why I didn't visit more often.

How can you apply this concept?

_____
_____
_____
_____
_____

Practice Microconnections Every Day

You may have heard the term "microaggression"—a form of bullying defined as brief exchanges that send denigrating messages to individuals because of their group membership. I believe we can broaden the definition to include any subtle bullying—eye-rolling after someone's comment, verbal digs and zings, ignoring someone's comments, and other disparagements. These can happen even when both parties are part of the same group.

We've all been on the receiving end of these kind of disrespectful encounters. They are designed to dismiss us, put us down, and signal we don't have value. Some of us have even perpetrated these, perhaps when younger and not conscious of the effect they have on others.

> *Small kindnesses help salve wounds*

Because these slights are commonplace, I want to suggest we shift our focus to giving "microconnections." Even if you've never inflicted microaggressions on anyone, every day you encounter people who have emotional wounds from such affronts.

Small kindnesses help salve those wounds. These simple acts require presence and awareness. Holding a door for someone, looking someone in the eye and saying "Thank you very much" for some nice act, or returning the shopping cart for a fellow shopper. Telling a stranger how nice he looks, or how she's done a great job with her well-behaved child, or your appreciation for a service provider's stellar service.

Why the term "microconnection"? Because when you are focused on a simple kind act, you are connecting with the person. Just a simple, brief acknowledgement can boost someone's mood and self-esteem. You are affirming they have value and they matter.

You don't know what someone is dealing with that may have them feeling low. Or how your simple act may buoy their mood when someone next slams them. I remember when I was meeting a new date for the first time. We'd agreed to meet at a shopping center and spend the afternoon together window shopping and getting to know each other. I was early, so I browsed the jewelry counter. An older woman shopper said to me, "I just want you to know how cute you look." I'm not used to strangers saying things like this to me so I asked her to repeat. She said it again.

With a new spring in my step, I alighted at the agreed-upon meeting spot. Within 10 minutes, my date said, "I'm going to go." I was surprised. I said, "Are you feeling OK?" He said, "Yes. I'm just not attracted to you."

Wow! At first it stung. But the kind woman's words rang in my ears. Soon I was laughing at how fortunate I was not to have wasted an afternoon with such an oaf!

It costs nothing to create a micro-connection. In fact, you may get a lot more back than you offer — a smile, hug, thank you, or memorable conversation. It's worth it even if you get nothing more than feeling great about spreading goodness.

About the Photo

My friend Holly lives 90 minutes north of San Francisco in the small seaside community of Gualala. Her home is on several acres of redwood groves and a creek.

Holly is a creative free spirit. With the help of her husband Bill, she's created a fairy forest. Yes, you read that right. A fairy forest.

Following a trail intersecting her property, Holly guided me to a dozen fairy villages with figurines illustrating the story she deftly and hilariously narrates. Holly has created a rich fantasy of these fairies' lives. I was never once bored during the hour-long tour.

We came to a redwood grove where a nearby prism cast its rainbow. The image was captivating, especially couched in the fairy lore. I had to capture it.

How can you apply this concept?

_____

_____

_____

_____

_____

Two Magic Words to Cool Tense Situations

Many disagreements are caused by misunderstandings. These can be as simple as someone not accurately hearing what the other said. Or they can be misinterpreting the other's actions in the worst possible way.

Two words can head off escalating the misunderstanding into a full-fledged argument, with loud voices, emphatic inflection, and accusatory words.

> *Being accusatory shuts down communication*

Instead of declaring inaccurate conclusions, condemning perceived motives, and mischaracterizing behaviors, try these two words instead.

"I'm confused."

Then calmly state what you thought you heard, saw or understood, owning that these are your experience, not declaring absolutely that this is what the other person did or said. Follow that with the possibility you could be in the wrong.

"I'm confused. I thought you said you'd deliver the report by this morning. Did I misunderstand?"

"I'm confused. My understanding was that you'd pay the bill no later than yesterday. Did you say something different?"

"I'm confused. My memory is that you said you'd have the sample by noon. Did I misremember or did something come up?"

"I'm confused. I thought we were jointly going to create the report. Did I miss your telling me you were going to do it on your own?"

Do you see how these comments state your understanding in a non-accusatory manner. You are not saying, "You said you'd deliver the report by this morning!" You are not adding, "Where is it?" or "You missed the deadline." or "You do this all the time." You're simply stating your understanding.

Then you follow up with a way for the other person to save face. Perhaps you did misunderstand. You are not saying that you are right. You're acknowledging there was a breakdown either in one or both of your understanding, or in follow through.

By saying, ""I'm confused," you're saying you want to discuss how your understanding is different than what you thought was going to happen. You're respectfully allowing the other person to explain his/her understanding and thinking.

These two words will create a respectful conversation and connection. Much more so than accusing and arguing.

About the Photo

I'm really lucky to know the renowned *National Geographic* photographer and speaker Dewitt Jones. When he was giving an iPhone photography class to a small group in South Lake Tahoe, I asked if there was an opening. There wasn't. I asked to be put on the waiting list. A week before the class started, he called to say there had been a cancelation and I was in! Luckily, it was a three-hour drive for me.

During the two days, Dewitt and his artist wife Lynette, showed the 20 of us in the class all sorts of cool tricks we could use to take better iPhone photos. We were mostly amateur photographers wanting to enhance our photos for ourselves.

However, Dewitt had arranged another professional photographer, Jack Davis, to be available to look at our photos and make suggestions. Jack is one of the top Photoshop experts in the world. Jack, Dewitt, and Lynette run photo workshops in Molokai, HI several times a year.

In addition to the technical information Dewitt shared, he did a session on his philosophy of photography. He said he strives to take at least one shot of beauty each day. He also illustrated a series of shots, each one more beautiful than the previous one. His point was to have patience, sit, observe, and capture what you find interesting. Chances are, others will, too.

After the class ended, I drove to Emerald Lake, not far from my hotel. I stopped to take photos of what caught my eye. The sun shining though this grove of redwoods seemed simple yet spectacular at the same time. Even more so after Jack made a few enhancements.

How can you apply this concept?

_____

_____

_____

_____

Waves Are Like People

The morning was spectacular—a warm Gulf breeze brushed my cheeks. Waves scampered across the beach.

Meditating on the waves' delicious sound, color and dance, I observed that even as they were approaching the shore, they were retreating.

A small berm lay between me and the surf. A few waves crossed the crest and scurried toward me. But most were spent before reaching the top.

I tried to discern which wave would make it over the top. At first, I thought I could tell by the size of the swell. Surely the largest would make it over. No.

Turning when I heard a loud crash, I thought, "That one will surely make it over." No.

Then it hit me.

These waves are like people. And the metaphor machine kicked into motion.

- ✦ Even as people move forward, progress is pitted with forces pulling us back. Sometimes we give into these forces when the pressure is too great. Sometimes we still progress despite the resistance.

- ✦ We never know what power is inside someone that propels them over the top. It's invisible. Sometimes the person isn't even aware it's there.

- ✦ People who come on the loudest, often don't have what it takes to ascend the crest.

- ✦ People who look like they have the power to make it, often don't. They may look like winners on the outside, but they are missing the power inside to succeed.

    Achievers are often quiet in their pursuits. We wouldn't necessarily predict that they were going to make it.

Life Is a Self-Designed, Personal Growth Seminar

About the Photo

Dewitt and Lynette led their iPhone photo class students to Lake Tahoe's shore to capture some sunset shots. We arrived an hour before the sun would dip behind the Sierra Nevada.

While we waited for the sky to change, we experimented shooting whatever was nearby: colorful kayaks stacked on the beach, a bride and bridegroom posing for photos, a ferry docked at the pier, and waves.

The lake is known for its deep blue color and it's clarity. The waves along the beach showed the water's transparency, exposing the brown, pebbled beach below.

The long shadow from the late-afternoon sun illuminated the waves in an uncommon way. I liked the contrast of the dark shadow with the white foam and the brown sand. From my vantage point on the pier, I could catch the shot at an unconventional angle.

One of the advantages of taking a class like Dewitt and Lynette's iPhoto one is the instructors encourage you to experiment and adopt a new perspective. This is how we grow in life — continually seeking new outlooks.

How can you apply this concept?

_____

_____

_____

_____

_____

A Formula for Growth

Most people would agree with Browning. Unfortunately, growth doesn't always come easily; often we feel "stuck." If you're feeling stuck, here's a formula to help you get unstuck:

Awareness

Awareness is the knowledge of our strengths, weaknesses, goals, and desires. As we become aware, the picture becomes clear. Vaguely amorphous feelings become focused and gain power, much as a ray of morning light broadens into day..

We increase awareness through introspection, creativity, classes and workshops, counseling, reading, and honest talks with friends, family, co-workers, even bosses. Awareness is a process, rather than a goal.

The force of awareness carries its own motivation. For example, a smoker who experiences severe chest pains (awareness) may quit smoking with surprising ease. If the stakes are high enough, we translate awareness into action, e.g., growth, without much discipline.

More often than not, however, the immediate stakes are not so high, so obvious or so tangible that awareness creates action. More often, we see the wisdom of changing our behavior while we continue our old patterns.

+ Self-Discipline

To break out of old patterns we need discipline. Athletes have coaches and musicians have teachers to provide both awareness and discipline. Most of the time, though, you're on your own.

How can you be your own coach? Begin by focusing on your goal, visualizing the outcome, and creating a plan (e.g., start with manageable steps, write them down, and keep promises made to yourself). You might enlist a friend as a surrogate coach to help you stay on track.

But sometimes nothing seems to work. No matter what you do, you remain stuck in old patterns. How do you know when to give up? When the effort is not worth the payoff? When your progress isn't commensurate with the time you spend? Or maybe you never give up.

= Growth

We don't achieve every goal we set for ourselves, but we can grow from every attempt we make—no matter what the outcome. For this reason our formula does not equal "success" or "results." We won't always succeed. However, if we choose, we can grow to a new level of wisdom.

> *We like the feeling of growth*

The formula itself isn't magic. It is, however, a shorthand method to help us remember why we put ourselves through painful and difficult situations, and why we deny ourselves certain pleasures. We like the feeling of working through the equation. We like the feeling of growth. We like knowing that we are better than we were before.

Life Is a Self-Designed, Personal Growth Seminar

About the Photo

I jumped at the chance to ride in a hot air balloon in Mandalay, Myanmar. I invited Christie, one of our group, to join me. She'd never been in a balloon before.

We arose before dawn for our 4:00 a.n. pickup. When we arrived at the closed old airport, we were surprised to see ours was the only balloon taking off that morning.

We snaked on pastries and juice as the ground crew busily readied the balloon. There were only two other passengers on this voyage. Soon we were aloft, taking in the pre-dawn sights.

Floating a few hundred feet over the old runway, we noticed a line of burgundy dots moving in a line across the landing field. Our pilot, Bill, said it was monks starting their rounds of collecting rice from the residents for their breakfast.

We quietly drifted over the city as it awoke early on this Sunday. We we're much higher than some of the apartment buildings. Looking down, we saw children so we waived, and greeted them with "manglaba" or hello in Myanmar. They delightedly returned our greeting.

Bill took us out over the river, where we came so close to a barge, I thought he was planning to land on it. Then he turned on the burners and we floated high above it.

Too soon, we landed on an island next to a monastery. The monks sat on their compound's wall and the village children came to watch us land. We walked to our waiting van with a parade of children at our side. It was another magical flight.

How can you apply this concept?

_____

_____

_____

_____

_____

Couple Candor with Kindness

Candor can be a wonderful gift. In its absence, many people think they are doing well, when really they are alienating others right and left. In consulting with managers for three decades, I've seen as much dysfunction resulting from no candor as from too much.

When feeling compelled to deliver unpleasant feedback, it is common to preface it with "I just want to be honest." That seems to then release the giver from any need to couch the comments in a way that takes into consideration how their words might affect the receiver. They can spew forth any judgmental and over arching comments in the delusion that they are being helpful.

More often then not, this candor is really an excuse to tell the receiver off, or share their perception of the person which isn't necessarily shared by anyone else.

The result is the receiver can get defensive or hurt. They can lash out, or withdraw, feeling that they have no redeeming qualities.

What's missing in the vast majority of cases is kindness. If the comments are delivered with some thought about timing, location and word choice, the message is much more likely to be heard and received. The receiver can then decide what actions, if any, are warranted.

The next time you feel you need to give some honest feedback, take some time to think through how you will say it, as well as when and where. You are more likely to make a difference with the receiver rather than alienate them.

About the Photo

Our Together We Can Change the World group was visiting NGO projects we support that serve impoverished women and children. We had to secure special government permission as we were entering areas not usually open to foreigners.

Our inn was situated on the Hpa-An River, in Hpa-An, Myanmar, a six-hour drive due east from Yangon (formerly Rangoon). At the end of a long, hot day visiting our projects, we were rewarded with a spectacular sunset.

A lone boatman set out as dusk descended. The river was still so his wake gently flowed behind him. The peacefulness was broken only by roosters occasionally crowing. The tiny mosquitos were out in force. Even with heavy-duty repellent, it made lingering outside unpleasant. After photographing the boatman for a few minutes, I retreated inside. The photo opportunity was then lost, but I'd captured some good shots.

Sometimes you have to suffer a bit for your art.

Resources

Go to RebeccaMorgan.com to access a variety of useful resources.

Speaking, Training, Consulting

Engage Rebecca to help your team more effective. Topics are detailed at the website.

Management Articles

Over 500 useful articles designed to help you manage your situations better.

Managers Discussion Guide Program

This program enables you to make your staff meetings come alive in 20-30 minutes per month, with no prep by you!

Books, MP3s and Learning Tools

High-quality tools to help you work more effectively.

Blog

At www.GrowYourKeyTalent.com read new ideas and stories to grow your key talent.

If you want more information on Together We Can Change the World, go to www.twcctw.org. Donations of any amount are appreciated.